Suomi Specialties

SUOMI SPECIALTIES

Finnish Celebrations
Recipes and Traditions

by
Sinikka Grönberg Garcia

Dedicated to all my grandchildren, especially Niko, Amanda, Kira, Marissa, Kevin, Emily, and Dominic, who were born after publication of The Finn in Me, *that you may cherish, always, the Finn in you.*
— Sinikka Grönberg Garcia

Associate editors: Joan Liffring-Zug Bourret,
    Melinda Bradnan, Dorothy Crum
Graphics editor: Walter Meyer
Illustrator: Jukka Mannio lives in Espoo and works for an advertising firm in Helsinki. He continues to study as he works in his chosen field.

Front cover: Sinikka Garcia is pictured in traditional dress of the Kaukola province, one of the sixteen Karelian provinces. The vest of dark blue wool cloth has pewter buttons and is decorated with red wool yarn embroidery along the edges ending in six yellow and red tassels. It is fastened with a brass hook. The dark blue wool skirt has a braid of red wool yarn encircling the hem. The blouse, with poet's sleeves, has an inset of handmade lace from the shoulder to the elbow. The apron, trimmed with handmade lace, has insets of lace between the stripes. The silver brooch, with dainty engravings, has a head with red and black ribbons sewn together at the top and pewter spikes attached. Sinikka holds a cone-shaped birch bark horn that resembles those used by shepherds (children) in early days.

Photography: Joan Liffring-Zug Bourret

© 1998 Sinikka Grönberg Garcia
ISBN 1-57216-039-X
Library of Congress 98-65711

THE AUTHOR
Sinikka Grönberg Garcia

Even after forty years in the United States, Sinikka Garcia still claims to be mostly a Finn. Content in Arizona, she still yearns for Finland, where her Finnish family lives. She has kept her Finnish language fluent by speaking as well as reading and writing in Finnish. She maintains an interest in Finnish folklore, particularly as it appears in the *Kalevala,* as well as in politics, the people, the changing language, nature and the environment, through frequent trips and keeping in a close touch with friends and relatives in Finland.

Following World War II, in 1951 Sinikka was a volunteer in the international work camp program initiated by the American Friends Service Committee (Quakers). The purpose of the camps was to foster international understanding as well as to provide physical help in needy areas of the world. For example, in Finland, clearing land was a great need since the government of Finland had granted land to men who had fought Finland's wars. Sinikka notes, "We yanked out stumps of trees with crowbars….We also sawed down smaller trees, did haying…mingled with the villagers." In Germany they assisted in the construction of a school for refugee children; in New Mexico, they helped construct a community center. The young men in a Mexican camp in the tropics brought potable water to the area, while the young women assisted medical personnel vaccinating children in rural areas.

It was at this camp that Sinikka met her husband Agustin. Sinikka and another volunteer, the only two who spoke Spanish, started a kindergarten class for children. "Chico" (Agustin) assisted as mentor as well as musician. Following an international courtship, Sinikka returned to the state of Tlaxcala in Mexico. In 1958, they immigrated to the United States, with son Quique, and settled in Tucson.

Sinikka has a bachelor of arts and a master's degree in education (with a minor in Spanish) from the University of Arizona. She taught for twenty-five years in Tucson's Catalina Foothills District, as well as in two programs at the university. The Garcias have four grown children: twin daughters who are teachers and two sons who are engineers. These days Sinikka's life is enhanced by her twelve grandchildren, who are a big part of her life.

After retiring, Sinikka wrote her memoirs in the book *The Finn In Me* published by North Star Press. She served on the Board of Directors of the annual "FinnFest U.S.A." from its founding till 1995. This endeavor sparked the Finnish-American Club of Tucson, of which she and her family have been members for over thirty years. Having served in most positions on the board, she is now editor of the newsletter, and wrote the club's thirty-year history.

Sinikka has translated two books of Tucson's history, *Pioneers in the Desert,* and *Outposts in the Desert* by Virginia C. Roberts, from English to Spanish for the largest school district in Tucson.

Knowing several true Finnish Americans — old-timers with heavy accents and pioneer lives — and having friends who are third or fourth generation Finns, has tremendously enriched her life. Sinikka has attended many "FinnFest" celebrations, and says that this renewal of friendships and Finnish-American culture sustains her through the year.

CONTENTS

Map of Finland 8
The Finnish People and Their Language 9
Becoming a Finnish American 10
A National Celebration: Independence Day 17
Holiday Celebrations 23
    Christmas in Finland 23
    New Year's Eve 31
Special Celebrations 35
    Loppiainen — Epiphany 35
    Laskiainen — Shrovetide 36
    Kalevala Day 38
    Easter 39
    Vappu — May Day 42
    Mother's Day 45
    Juhannus — Midsummer 46
    St. Urho's Day 49
Customs 54
    At a Memorial Service 54
    Nimipäivä — Name Day 58
    A Summer Wedding 60
    Talkoot — "Working Bees" 62
    The Sauna 65
    The Summer Cottage Syndrome 68
Finland Society — *Suomi Seura R.Y.* 70
    "FinnFest" 72
    Finnish American Club of Tucson 75
Traveling in Finland 77
Festivals in Finland 85
Medieval Churches in the Finnish Southwest 106
The Evangelical Lutheran Church of Finland 111
Finland Now and in the Twenty-First Century 114

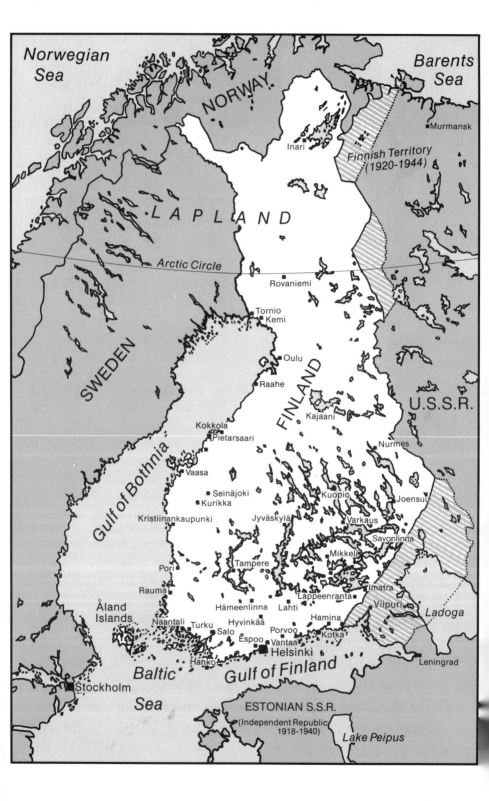

THE FINNISH PEOPLE
and Their Language

The Finns have survived conquests and domination by the Swedes, the Russians, and indirectly by the Danes when the thrones of Norway, Denmark and Sweden were united. There is evidence of inhabitants in Finland 9000 years ago. According to experts who met in the Ugrian World Congress in Finland in 1995, Finnish genes are mostly from the Baltic-Germanic gene pools — 75 percent of them. The rest, along with the Finnish language roots, come from the East.

The cradle of the Finns stretched from the Volga River to the British Isles. To summarize briefly, suffice it to say that Finland was a part of Sweden for 600 years, and a Grand Duchy under several Russian czars for a hundred years. Among the northern countries, Finland and Iceland are republics whose head is a president; Sweden, Norway, and Denmark are constitutional monarchies with a queen or king at the throne. The countries share a common past in the Swedish empire. You can get by speaking Swedish in all of them, and, nowadays, English. The Swedish language is still the second official language in Finland, and many Finns have Swedish surnames.

The Finnish language is a unique phenomenon — totally different from the languages of the aforementioned countries. It originated east of the Ural Mountains, but is intermingled with words borrowed from Indo-European, from the Baltic and Germanic languages, and from Russian. Perhaps that is the reason Finland is not always, in spite of its location, considered a Scandianavian country. Finland was never occupied by the Soviet Union, but fought for independence in 1939-1940 and 1941-1944, and was able to keep it.

Becoming a Finnish American

Among the first generation of Finns in America there is a strong reluctance to being labeled "Finnish American." You are a Finn and want to remain one for a long time. After all, you didn't come here to escape poverty or to avoid being drafted into the Russian Army. You came as a visitor, as a bride or groom, an au pair, or an exchange student on a scholarship. You came to learn the language. You did not need to leave Finland.

You resist the change and remain a Finnish citizen, even though you hold a "green card." You may give up your original citizenship in order to teach in the U.S. public school system, as I did in 1964. I tried to "not think about it." I was still a Finn, married to another foreigner. Three of our four children were born Americans, except the oldest, born in Mexico, remained a Mexican citizen until my husband changed his citizenship.

As a newcomer to this country, you keep in constant touch with your folks in Finland by writing and telephoning news. They send subscriptions to magazines and the *Helsingin Sanomat*. You want to travel to Finland every summer, no matter what cost. Then, as your children get established in their school environment, you open up and get to know their friends and families. Life does go on!

How I Became A Finnish American

One day a visiting relative ran into an American Finn at the post office as she was mailing a letter to Finland. We were all invited to the *Juhannus* celebration of the Finnish-American Club of Tucson. A new era began when we became members. We joined the others in singing *"Maamme"* with great respect and misty eyes. I got to know three "old timers" — three Finnish-American women, who enriched my life and that of my family. They were Hilda Mankwell, Eeva Siltala and Hilja Saari — all of them now gone. Each was born in Finland in the previous century, and each one was a storehouse of pioneer immigrant experience in these United States.

At first I was amused by the sound of old-fashioned Finnish and Finglish, which is a mixture of old Finnish and bad English. Once in awhile my ears hurt — as when hearing a scraping sound — when words like *nisu* or "biscuit" were used instead of the bread's "proper" name *pulla* (which comes from Swedish *bullan*). Yet, somehow it was sad when, in the 70s, our club dropped the Finglish from its meeting minutes. By then it had actually become entertaining to hear the text read.

There was a limbo period in my Finnishness, when I "was nothing." Slowly, due to the influence of the club, almost unnoticed I "let go" and got involved in activities and become attached to people like the three dear ladies mentioned earlier.

Through my new Finnish-American friends, I learned about the lives of immigrants who came to America in the early part of the 19th century, about the Finn Halls, the Temperance Societies, the Lutheran Church, and the different groups into which Finnish immigrants divided.

I continued in my new club, and after becoming a board member and being elected to different positions year after year, I got a fuller picture. I needed new sources of inspiration to reintroduce our club to modern-day happenings in Finland. A 1977 visit by the head of the *Suomi Seura* (Finland Society) — Tauri Aaltio himself — gave the needed boost.

At the suggestion of Tauri Aalto, our group organized a concert by a folksinger from Finland, Barbara Helsingius. Our club met other ethnic groups in town and expanded activities, for instance, the community fair "Tucson Meet Yourself." Later when elected a member of the "FinnFest U.S.A." Board, I experienced the richness of the first "FinnFest" in 1983 — a big step toward becoming a Finnish American! I was revitalized and understood the importance of knowing my identity as a Finnish American — a recognizable strand in the tapestry of ethnicity in America. I learned that the so-called "melting pot" theory was just that — a theory. The melting doesn't really happen; I didn't completely "melt."

One day I discovered that many of the founders of our club had been quietly passing away. At these memorial services, with Finnish hymns and the group singing Finnish songs, I felt united in my ethnicity.

Many new people entered the club, some of them coming directly from Finland, bringing a fresh breath to the club's activities. We write plays, perform singing in and outside the club, and enjoy our Finnish music greatly.

At some point, I realized that I had not been keeping up-to-date on the composition of the Finnish Parliament, or that I wasn't very interested in the issues, such as Karelia's future. And those Finns still holding onto a Finnish passport, hardly bother to travel to Los Angeles to cast their vote in Finnish elections! Another sign of "getting there" was an increasing interest in the Finnish-American newspapers: *Raivaaja, Amerikan Uutiset, Finnish American Reporter.*

Becoming Aware

Finnish-American communities have changed with the times. Older generations, with their rusty Finnish-Finglish have passed on. Events at the "FinnFests" are conducted in English. It seems that being Finnish American does not have to include the Finnish language, but what about the teachings of the 19th-century Fennoman A.I. Arwidsson? He wrote, "A nation possesses, as a unique treasure, its language, which in its mythical way interprets its special traits. The national legacy lives within the language itself." Distance from the mother country makes it harder for American Finns to define their legacy.

Of course, Finnish Americans showed a strong patriotism for Finland during the hard times of her wars. They rose to the occasion by sending clothing, food and money to Finland in the 40s. They even paid for chartered air transportation!

In the 60s, the Finnish airline Finnair, assisted by Hanslin Travel Service, started group trips *(Seuramatkoja)* to Finland. Our first trip in 1965 was on an Icelandic Airlines' propeller aircraft that needed refueling in Reyjavik. Today Finnair flies nonstop from both coasts. Finnair also assists many Finnish-American projects financially, and has a chorus that performs at "FinnFests." Visiting Finland has become a habit for many Finnish Americans; relationships are renewed, and new bonds are created.

Although the era of the great Finn Halls, the era of expression and entertainment that tied the Finnish-American community together is over, there are still many strongholds of Finnish-American activity around, for example: Fitchburg, Massachusetts, Virginia, Minnesota, Lantana-Lake Worth, Florida, and Sonoma, California. Many of these have large memberships and still have a hall where great cultural programs — lectures, plays, concerts — are performed by community members and by visiting Finnish and Finnish-American performers. Sports events may take place there also.

There is the *Suomi Koulu* (Finnish School sponsored by the Finnish government) program for children, usually taught Saturdays in different Finnish-American communities.

At the university level, the study of the Finnish language has increased; for instance, there is a Finnish Studies program with a Finnish government professorship at the University of Minnesota. An ongoing project called Reunion Sisters researches and teaches Finnish interests. Marianne Wargelin-Brown, a pillar of the Finnish-American community, is a leader in the Sisters' project. There is much involvement in Finnish studies and Finnish immigrant collections at the Immigrant History Research Center at the University of Minnesota.

Both Finnish and American special occasions are celebrated in hundreds of Finnish-American communities. *Juhannus* or "Midsummer" festival and "Little Christmas" in the beginning of December are the most celebrated of all. There are other special celebrations and happenings that have not made their way to this continent (see "Special Celebrations"), and one celebration of Finnish-American origin is not celebrated in Finland — St. Urho's Day on the16th of March. (See "St. Urho's Day").

THE FINLAND SOCIETY

Involvement as a Finnish American started for me within the Finland Society — *Suomi Seura* — in Helsinki in 1982, where the idea of a Finnish-American "FinnFest" was born. The Society has been a true supporter as well as donor of funds and prizes ever since. It sponsors many special projects including: an annual Finnish Language and Culture Seminar for young people from all over the world; it publishes *Suomen Silta* magazine six times a year; it gives scholarships and grants to students and organizations. As one of the official programs of Finland's 80th Anniversary, the Finland Society sponsored a preliminary session for an Expatriate Parliament, encouraging all Finnish organizations abroad to send a representative. This session was to lay a foundation for the parliament itself. The character of the Finland Society has been changing with the times. Its Golden Age was in the 80s; now new members are welcomed to meet the challenge of change.

PROJECT 34

Project 34 helps 3rd and 4th generations of American Finns to preserve their roots and to enjoy Finnish culture. Founded in Dallas, the group is directed by John Laine, a Texas-Finn. Concerns are youth involvement, improving communication between local organizations, and accessing Finnish materials.

SALOLAMPI

Salolampi is the Finnish Language Village located near Bemidji on Turtle River Lake in Minnesota. Sponsored and operated by Concordia College, Moorhead, children learn Finnish culture and language in the summer. It has Finnish-design log cabins and the main house, *Jyringintalo,* is modeled after the railway station in Jyväskylä, Finland. The Finnish style surroundings were built by generous donations from the Salolampi Foundation. The language is learned by speaking it in daily life. You "buy" (Finnish money) and "eat" in Finnish. There is a sauna and lake for swimming; kantele playing and rag-rug weaving; singing and dancing. Programs held during "Adult Weeks" appeal to adults. Scholarships are available.

THE FINLANDIA FOUNDATION, INC.

The Finlandia Foundation, Inc. has chapters nationwide. It promotes a variety of projects including: scholarships for studying in Finland and in the U.S.A., trust awards for academic research and education, chapter projects, music, Finnish-American Visual Arts — films, theater and other performances. It chooses and supports a "Finnish-American Artist of the Year." Bernhard Hillila, retired professor and author of several books including *FinnFun,* was the 1997 recipient of this award. It also supports heritage projects, the publishing and translating of Finnish literature, and the Language Camp, *Salolampi.*

FINNISH-AMERICAN TRANSLATORS' ASSOCIATION

The Finnish-American Translators' Association makes Finnish literature available to those who do not know Finnish. Literature of Finnish interest is kept alive by an amazing number of excellent Finnish-American writers and poets. FATA strives to promote and improve translations from Finnish. Through its efforts, Finnish is the only so-called minor language for which the nation-wide American Translators' Association offers an accreditation examination.

SUOMI COLLEGE

Founded over a hundred years ago in Hancock, Michigan, Suomi College has a full three-year baccaluareate program and works with the Finnish Kuopio Academy of Crafts and Design; they exchange teachers and students. Also at Suomi is The Finnish American Heritage Center that collects and preserves Finnish-American archives, which are available to all researchers.

A National Celebration

INDEPENDENCE DAY

Between "Little Christmas" and Christmas, on December 6th, is Finland's Independence Day. This is a proud occasion celebrating independence gained in 1917. There are parades, flags, bands, patriotic speeches, formal and informal gatherings including a ball at the presidential palace with honored guests. It is the biggest event in presidential circles, and a big media event. All who have found fame during the year either in the arts, industry or sports are invited. The presidential ball might be considered Finland's answer to the "Oscars" night in Hollywood; even the gowns worn by the celebrities seem to be the object of utmost curiosity to all.

All over the country, in almost every household, two blue-and-white candles are placed on the window sill and lit in the afternoon since the short winter day is dark by three p.m. The national hymn *"Maamme"* (Our Land) is played over the radio and television, and patriotic programs are broadcast. The message of the broadcast touches on the hard-won wars for liberty — costs and problems. In a small nation patriotic feelings are easily aroused; everyone has been touched by sacrifice and loss, and all enjoy, with pride, the glory of their beloved Finland.

A typical observance of this national holiday by Finnish Americans follows:

**The Celebration of Finland's 80th Anniversary
December 6, 1997
by the Finnish American Club, Tucson, Arizona**

There were two traditional blue-and-white candles peacefully glowing at the front of the room, as well as the two countries' flags standing tall. There was a patriotic speech by one of the members, a proud young man from Finland, telling the story of his country. *"Maamme"* (Our Land) was sung:

Maamme
The National Anthem by J.L. Runeberg
Translated by Clement B. Shaw

"Our land, our land, our fatherland,
Sound loud, O name of worth!
No mound that meets the heaven's band
No hidden vale, no wave-washed strand,
Is loved as is our native North,
Our own forefathers' earth."

*"Oi maamme Suomi synnyinmaa,
Soi sana kultainen!
Ei laaksoa, ei kukkulaa,
Ei vettä, rantaa rakkaampaa.
Kuin kotimaa tää pohjoinen,
Maa kallis isien."*

The play "The Evacuees" was performed by fifteen members, ranging in age from six years old to almost eighty. I wrote the play at the suggestion of the play's director. My husband provided the props, making a huge oven-stove structure of refrigerator boxes, and a grandfather clock to measure time. There hung a *täkänä,* a *ryijy*-rug woven by my sister, on the wall; an oil lamp and a birch bark basket on the table, a rag rug on the floor, and two shiny copper coffee pots on the stove. We made sure we clicked the coffee cups once in a while. As "Hanna," I was knitting a mitten with five knitting needles whenever there was a chance, and "Antti," the head of the household and farmer, whittled an ax handle in the opening scene. When the narrator mentioned "men turned soldiers marching," a powerful Finnish march (*"Nuijamiesten marssi"*) was played. As the narrator was summarizing the story toward the end, Jean Sibelius's "Finlandia" was heard first softly, then louder. Here are the program notes:

THE EVACUEES
by Sinikka G. Garcia

A play based on my real life experiences as an eight-year-old during the evacuation of the Karelians at the start of the Winter War in 1939-40. The idea for this play came from Kathi M. Lucey, program director, who suggested that I take something about the war from my book *The Finn In Me.* So, I did, reliving the events and remembering the people important to us, especially Hanna and Antti Massinen, during the Winter War of 1939-1940.

The First Scene deals with the unexpected arrival of Mailis and her three children from Värtsilä in Finland's Karelia, in

Massilanmäki, a small farming community in Savo, just west of Savonlinna. Mailis had convinced a few military officers to let her family get on their military train that was going west. Hundreds of other evacuees were left behind.

The Second Scene introduces "Juutti," a neighbor, who brings the latest news to the Massinens. The first news is of the bombing of the very train of evacuees that Mailis and her children had been on. News of the war comes in Juutti's reports and from the visit by Laura, an Army nurse on furlough, and by Kalle, a wounded young soldier on sick leave.

Scene Three welcomes more evacuees — old folks and children — into the Massinen household. Families came, with their starving and freezing animals, from even more eastern villages. The children, especially, tell about their experiences encountered on the way: of burning villages, bombings, gunfire, dying animals, and Finnish speaking spies.

In the Fourth Scene, Juutti brings very bad news of Finland's accepting the terms of Moscow for a truce. The Russians were an overwhelming force with their superior weaponry and endless armies. The Finns fought "with religious fervor" and retained their independence. They held out longer than any expert had ever calculated, but at the end of the war, 11 percent of Finland had been lost and 400,000 evacuees were homeless.

The play ends as the evacuees leave in search of a new life under new circumstances including the burden of an enormous war debt to the Russians. Finland, absolutely united, picks up the pieces and readies for the gigantic task ahead — and for a Continuation War a year later.

Celebrate with Traditional Foods

Along with shared interest in a cause for celebration, bonds are formed by sharing traditional foods. A suggestion for this occasion is *Karjalan Piirakkas* (Rice Pies). The *piirakkas* are not a dessert, but are a favorite snack and a tasty item for a Finnish buffet. Of Karelian (eastern Finland) origin, their use spread during World War II. After the Russians took Karelia in 1940, 400,000 Karelian evacuees had to be accomodated all over Finland. Now *piirakkas* are well-known in every Finnish province.

It used to be a sign of the most competent baker to make *piirakkas;* for instance, my mother never dared make them because my grandmother was the designated *piirakka*-maker. In Tucson, among our Finnish Club members, we developed a system that allows anybody to succeed in the *piirakka*-making. Instead of individually rolling each *piirakka* shell — an impossible task if trying to get each the same size — we roll the dough as if making gingerbread cookies. Then with a small demitasse saucer, we cut circles of the dough — they all turn out almost identical in size. The thickness of the dough can vary, but about 1/8 inch is ideal. You get 24-26 *piirakkas* from the following recipe. You can wrap them either in plastic wrap for freezing or for heating later in a microwave oven, or foil for heating in a regular oven. Delicious served with butter on top!

Karjalan Piirakkas — Karelian Rice Pies

For the dough:
1 1/2 cups white flour	2 Tbsp. oil
1 1/2 cups rye flour	1 cup water
	1 tsp. salt

Filling:
3 cups milk	1 tsp. salt
3 cups water	1 Tbsp. butter/margarine
(or milk)	1 cup long grain rice

Filling: Bring water or milk to a boil; add salt and butter. Lower temperature and add the rice, stirring often. Cook about one-half hour. Let cool.

Dough: Mix flours and salt. Add the oil, water and milk. Stir and knead gently, adding flour if necessary for a solid ball. Form a stick (about 1 foot long) on a floured board and divide it into four equal parts. Roll each part to a thickness of about 1/8 inch. Turn and add flour underneath to avoid sticking. Cut out as many circles as you can, reworking left-over dough. Place on an ungreased cookie sheet. Preheat oven to 450°.

Assembly: Place a serving spoon full of filling in the center of each circle, spreading it a little. Fold the left and right sides toward the center, not quite touching. Using the thumb and forefinger of each hand, pinch both edges into the rice simultaneously from the middle to the ends, shaping into a "boat." Make sure the filling is showing in the middle.

Bake at 450° for about 15 minutes until light brown. Remove from oven and baste with melted butter or margarine. If you prefer soft *piirakkas,* cover them.

Note: Unbaked *piirakka* dough should not be saved to another day, because it becomes viscous.

Holiday Celebrations

CHRISTMAS IN FINLAND

Long before Christmas, late in October when it's dark and rainy most of the time in Helsinki, we started our Christmas shopping. We covered our faces against the wind, at times walking backwards as we struggled to "Tempo," our favorite dimestore by the Siltasaari Bridge. Everything was bright and inspiring there. We had saved some money and were very willing to spend it on others. However, the only thing I ever remember buying was a plate, with dainty lilac flowers on its slightly scalloped rim, for my mother. It cost 20 marks in 1942, and is still in the family.

One of the before-Christmas activities was baking gingerbread cookies in very crowded conditions in our small kitchen. (This was war time with housing shortages. We were Karelian refugees.) I remember the time when Pentti, our little brother, was baking with us and discovered that his left arm was good for transporting cut-out cookies onto the cookie sheet!

Before many a Christmas in the early 40s, I sold Christmas magazines door-to-door in our building to earn Christmas money. We made table decorations with lingonberry stems and pine cones, which we sprayed with white foam for snow. We sat around the table when Dad was writing Christmas cards; we chose the cards for each family. I also wrote cards and delivered them myself to friends. It was exciting to hear the mail chute creak and the mail drop on the floor.

The forerunner for Christmas is "Little" Christmas, which coincides with the first Advent around the end of November and beginning of December. The hymn *"Hoosianna Davidin poika..."* is sung in all churches — a true spirit-lifting occasion in the country — and the first Advent candle is lit. The main street, Alexander Street, gets its Christmas lights and decorations, and people go out to enjoy the display windows and the lights. The period before Christmas is the time for parties. Refreshments are served and perhaps small presents are exchanged among friends. In America, the Finnish Americans go all out for a Little Christmas (*Pikkujoulu*) party; there's often a Finnish dinner, Finnish music, a play, elf dances, a lot of singing, and Santa appears with gifts for the children.

Nowadays electric Christmas lights have taken the place of real candles on the Christmas tree, eliminating the tradition of actually sitting down to "watch the tree" each time the candles were lit. You couldn't leave them burning unattended; that's why you watched them. It was a special moment of enjoyment for the family while sipping and tasting something delicious from the table. One of the children might even have the honor of lighting the candles.

Getting a tree from the woods was the custom in the country. In the city, you made the trip to a tree lot with your father, and carried the tree home the evening of December 23. The tree was brought in on Christmas Eve day, and was decorated after Father came home from work, around noon. Father would place the tree on its stand, put the candles in their holders, clip or tie them onto the strongest branches — a very difficult job to keep them pointing up — and place the star at the top. We children did the rest, including the hanging of tinsel, apples, and the colorful strings of Scandinavian flags. During this time or soon after, the whole family would pause to listen to the declaration of "Christmas peace" message coming through radio from Turku Cathedral, along with the sound of the cathedral bells. It is an old, respected custom, ending in "and now it is Christmas." It is understood that the declaration carries a penalty for breaking the Christmas peace, and every year it sends goose bumps over you.

A visit to the cemetery where family and relatives lie, breaks up the afternoon of Christmas Eve day, which seems endless to the children. Candles are lit and red tulips in birch bark containers are placed on the snow-covered tombs. The cemetery is aglow with these candles, resembling a sea of light against the dark tombstones and the gray sky. It is a quieting moment before the gaiety of Christmas Eve itself.

Mother is busy cooking the ham and casseroles. It's been a hectic time for her with the baking and the cleaning and everything else. She wishes the children to vanish from underfoot. If the weather is good, and there is snow on the ground, the children go skiing or sledding. Unfortunately snow doesn't always cover the land at Christmastime; there are many rainy Christmas seasons.

A wonderful smell fills the house! By six o'clock the table is set, and then the food is brought in — ham and boiled potatoes, rutabaga casserole, specially sweetened potato casserole, *rosolli* (a salad with beets, potatoes, carrots and herring), and lingonberry relish. There is a variety of breads in the basket. For dessert there is steaming-hot rice pudding, and fruit soup.

Soon after dinner is over and the dishes taken away, the waiting intensifies. Christmas music and programs are on the radio, but most of all we are waiting to hear a knock on the door. This was the tradition until the year I was fifteen, my brother Juhani was thirteen; my sister Anja, ten, and our littlest brother Pentti, four years old. For his sake we had played the game of pretending Father Christmas *(joulupukki),* who came to our house with sacks full of gifts, was real. When he passed out the gifts, he read each name and questioned each one of us. We swore we had been good all year and we sang a song. It was at this Christmas that Pentti began to wonder about Santa's "wooden" face. After Santa (Father Christmas) left, we tore open the packages — the best part. Each year we all received books and clothing, skis or sleds, and the younger ones got toys. One Christmas I got a two-layer xylophone that I loved, and another time, a thick diary that today contains precious material ending in 1954. (I discovered it in 1973 in the attic of my parents' home.)

Before we retired with our "loot," Mother would have the coffee table ready with goodies: braided cardamom *pulla* with raisins, cinnamon rolls, spice cake, sugar cake, gingerbread cookies that we ourselves had made, and a moist, raspberry-filled cake.

On Christmas morning some of us went to church where we sang "The angel of heaven declared this...Our Lord Jesus Christ was born today to us...and you can witness this when seeing this child sleeping in the manger." It is a wonderful hymn.

The rest of the day was quiet, except for the books and the games we loved to get into — "Monopoly," "Stock Market," and card games such as "Black Peter."

Boxing Day, December 26th, is a day for quiet play and visiting relatives and friends. Celebrated in most European countries, it is named from the traditional "giving of boxes" to servants in England. As we grew older, we would stay home and play while the rest of the family went visiting. We'd have friends over to play, light the candles on the tree, nibble on something good and enjoy our company.

Traditional Foods for the Season

I am a person who does not collect or try out new recipes, but the ones I use I know by heart. For forty years now, my family has enjoyed Finnish *pulla* — a braided yeast bread with cardamom and sometimes raisins — and each time it is well received. At first we baked it only at Christmastime; now we bake it more often. For the Finnish Club's Little Christmas party in early December, we make a *pulla* ring the size of the oven, placing it on aluminum foil and baking it directly on the grill. I say "we" because my husband Chico is the one who does the heaviest part of the *pulla;* he kneads it. He knows the process and when the loaves are ready for the oven. Everything is done from scratch; he does not use a bowl, but makes a "crater" of flour on the table and puts everything else in the middle of it. For others — I recommend a bowl!

The night before a baking session, I bring together all of the ingredients so they are at room temperature when the preparation starts. The next morning I mix the yeast in warm water, warm up the milk, crack the eggs, and grease the cookie sheets. I hand each ingredient to Chico as he mixes and kneads the dough into a smooth ball. I watch over the rising of the dough, glaze the loaves, preheat the oven, and supervise the baking — 10 to 12 loaves at a time.

A divine, sweet smell fills the house! After taking the loaves from the oven, I let them cool and glaze them once more. I start the coffee perking and savor the results of this labor of love that has taken at least five hours by now. I lift my legs up and enjoy a cup of freshly perked coffee (Chico has gone to work by then) and a generous hunk of *pulla* with butter melting on it.

There's one more phase to the *pulla* making — storing it. I usually cut cardboard to fit under each loaf, covering the boards with foil and the bread with plastic wrap. Adding a bow later makes a worthy Christmas gift. The baked loaves are easily frozen, or you can freeze any unbaked dough for another time, and handy gift-giving. So here goes:

Pulla — Yeast Cardamom Bread

1/2	cup warm water	2	cups sugar
3	envelopes dry yeast	2	bars margarine, melted
4	cups warm milk	7	eggs, beaten
1	tsp. salt	5	lbs. flour, or about 16 cups
1	tube fresh cardamom or 1 Tbsp. ground	2	eggs beaten with a little sugar for glazing

All ingredients should be at room temperature. Mix the yeast first in the warm water. Then in a large bowl mix everything except the flour. Slowly stir in the flour, kneading the dough by hand until evenly smooth and glossy. Wipe the surface of the dough with margarine (use margarine wrappers). Cover with plastic wrap and let rise at least an hour. When the dough has doubled, punch down and let rise again until about half as high. Preheat oven to 400°.

Divide dough into as many parts as you are making loaves. By hand, roll each part into three strands (an inch in diameter and about as long as the width of a cookie sheet) for each loaf (3 loaves per sheet). Braid the strands and glaze the loaves. Let rise. Just before putting them into the oven, glaze again. Bake the loaves at 400° for 20-25 minutes. Glaze the loaves once more. Let cool. Makes 10 to 12 loaves. Enjoy!

Note: This dough is also used for *korvapuustit* (cinnamon rolls), *laskiaispullat* (lenten rolls). When baking items smaller than the *pulla* loaf, lower the oven temperature.

Korvapuustit or Cinnamon Rolls

These figures look like an ear; that's why the name *korva* for "ear" and *puusti* for "striking on the ear."

pulla dough (for instance 1/4 of the above recipe)
cinnamon and sugar mixed
butter or margarine at room temperature
2 eggs beaten with a little sugar (for glazing)

Korvapuustit (Cinnamon Rolls) are individual buns made of *pulla* dough which is rolled out to a 1/4 inch thickness. On it butter or margarine is spread and a layer of cinnamon and sugar is sprinkled to cover it well. Roll up into a roll of about 2 1/2 inches in diameter. The roll is then cut into triangular portions, about 2 inches in size at the bottom. Starting at the top, each tip of the triangle is lifted up and pressed down crosswise, using two little fingers (tip to tip). This flattens the triangle exposing the layers of butter and cinnamon. Glaze the buns and let rise. Just before baking, glaze them again. Bake at 375° for about 15 minutes. Glaze again for a rich sheen.

Christmas Ham with Prunes
from *Fantastically Finnish*

1 fresh ham, 6 to 8 lbs.	1 (10 1/2 oz.) can beef consommé
20 pitted prunes	1 cup currant jelly
1 cup minced onion	1/2 cup orange juice
1/4 cup applesauce	1/2 cup port wine
1 1/2 cups pared, chopped apple	1/2 tsp. salt

Have butcher remove center bone from ham (fresh pork leg) and cut a deep pocket in the cavity. Coarsely chop the prunes; combine with onion, applesauce and chopped apple. Fill the cavity with apple mixture, overlap and tie with a string to secure ends. Score fat side of ham and place fat-side-up in shallow baking pan. Pour consommé over ham and roast at 325° (baste often) for 30 to 35 minutes per pound (to 170° on meat thermometer). Transfer ham to a serving platter. Remove fat from pan juices. Bring juices to a boil, stirring in browned bits, and boil to reduce juices (about 5 minutes). Stir in currant jelly, orange juice, port and salt. Simmer this sauce 10 to 15 minutes. To serve: remove string from ham, slice thinly. Serve sauce in a separate dish. Serves 6 to 8.

NEW YEAR'S EVE

There were New Year's Eves in my early life when my parents would go to the theater, leaving me alone at home with the younger children. The responsibility seemed great, and I recall worrying over my parents as well. What if something happened to them? What would I do? Listening to the ticking of the clock, I wished I could sleep like my sister and brothers. One time, as I listened to the radio news, I heard of the 50 percent devaluation of the Finnish mark! Your money and savings were worth one half of what they were worth the day before — I informed my parents of this when they came home that night!

The memorable and fun Eves were during my early teens, when my friends — all seven of us — joined the crowd at the steps of the Helsinki Cathedral (*Suurkirkko*). Facing the big square full of people, we sang to the accompaniment of the big Army band "God is our Castle, our eternal, strong protection..." while the cannons boomed. We listened to the speeches, felt patriotic pride, and enjoyed the fireworks shooting over the harbor. We walked home arm-in-arm in the cold night, inspired and in awe of the high dome of stars above us.

In keeping with another tradition, we spent several New Year's Eves, usually at our friend Inge's house, melting solder (tin) in a special dipper over an open fire, waiting for our turn to dump the liquefied metal into a bucketful of snow or cold water. The splash made steam and a loud thud as the metal hit the bottom of the bucket. As it hardened, it broke into so many pieces that you could hear dinging against the bucket. The biggest piece was then retrieved and dried, and placed in front of a light. Thus, a shadow formed on the wall, and it was studied and interpreted to predict your future! A ship or an airplane, of course, meant travel, and certain shapes predicted a boyfriend or husband, etc. The game was fun in any group. Even shy people could shine in it.

Another great New Year's Eve memory is of a pillow fight and an eleven egg cake that we beat by hand, all seven of us taking turns. While baking, the cake rose nicely; we kept opening the oven door to see it rise. All of a sudden, it flattened completely! A great disappointment, but we couldn't stop laughing, and some of us were rolling uncontrollably on the floor. Eleven eggs were a lot in the 40s when food shortages still existed. From our rations we had all contributed the ingredients for this infamous cake.

Later, New Year's Eves included young men in our company at our cabin, surrounded by snow, in the country. Dancing was one of the main attractions, as was the preparation of the meals and card playing. Thinking back, I always feel the presence of the winter sky with millions of stars that twinkle coldly and make you feel so small. *Hyvää Uutta Vuotta* to you!

Traditional Foods for the Season

A few years back, at a "FinnFest" food demonstration, I learned the English word for *vispipuuro:* "Air Pudding." It reminded me of a *Vispipuuro* happening in Finland.

My brother Juhani, my school friend Hellä and I had traveled to Uncle Arvi's at Imatra for skiing. To help Aunt Tyyne one evening, Hellä and I decided to make "Air Pudding" for dessert. Beating the pudding in a snowdrift was a memorable event. We took turns beating with a wire beater, anxiously waiting for it to cool and become fluffy. Our hands were freezing; it was cold and getting colder by the minute. The sun was an orange fireball — a huge disk ready to set on the western horizon; on the opposite side of the sky was a silvery moon — brilliant in the blue sky and very cold looking. The sight left us awe-struck. As we paused, turning our heads from one to the other, our breath formed little cloudlets around our eyes. It was as if we were squeezed between the sun and the moon with our pink pudding and freezing hands. Soon the pudding was fluffy, and we ran indoors with it. My five young cousins loved our pink Air Pudding!

Vispipuuro — Whipped Berry Pudding — Air Pudding

3 cups cranberry juice (or lingonberry)*	1/2 cup Cream of Wheat Sugar to taste (about 1/2 cup)

Bring the juice to boiling. Sprinkle Cream of Wheat in slowly, beating vigorously to avoid lumps. Cook slowly for about 1/2 hour. You'll be surprised at how the amount triples!

Pour the pudding into a large mixing bowl and whip at high speed until the texture is creamy, lighter colored and fluffy — about 20 minutes of beating. It takes longer by hand in the snowdrift. Add sugar as desired. Serve with sugar on top and with milk or cream. Makes 4 to 6 servings.

Other juices that are not as tangy can be used, but may need lemon juice added.

Another favored food for all seasons is *Kaalilaatikko* (Cabbage Casserole). Instead of making cabbage rolls, I, long ago, switched to Cabbage Casserole for the simple reason that my children would not eat the cabbage leaves outside the roll, yet, they would eat the chopped cabbage in the casserole. I accidentally put raisins in this dish once — as if making a liver-rice casserole — and the raisins then became a required ingredient. So this dish may be made with or without the raisins.

For the two of us, since the children are gone, I use the following recipe:

Kaalilaatikko — Cabbage Casserole

1 medium-sized cabbage	1 green pepper, chopped
Boiling water (reserve)	Salt and pepper to taste
1 lb. ground beef	Ground allspice to taste
1 cup uncooked rice	2 boullion cubes
1 large onion, chopped	2 cups reserved liquid
	Handful of raisins if desired

Cut cabbage into strips (1 inch wide), and cook in boiling water for about 2-3 minutes. Drain and reserve the liquid. Cover the bottom of oven dish with cabbage. Add a layer of ground meat, then a layer of rice. Over the layer of rice sprinkle chopped onions, green pepper, seasonings, and raisins if adding. Repeat layers as needed. Dissolve boullion cubes in the hot cabbage water and pour over the casserole. Cover with foil and bake at 375° for about 30 minutes. Remove foil and bake another 10 minutes, or until rice is done and top is browned. The top can be brushed with syrup which will give a nice color and flavor. In Finland this dish is served with lingonberry relish. Here in the U.S., I serve it with cranberry sauce.

Special Celebrations

LOPPIAINEN — EPIPHANY

The 6th of January is *Loppiainen* ("end" in Finnish) or Epiphany, which depicts the time when the three wise men with their gifts reached Bethlehem and the manger in which the Jesus child was found. This terminates Christmas festivities, and the Christmas trees come down with a small celebration! Families get together for the last lighting of the candles on the tree, then, respectfully, each decoration is taken down and put away in a box, and the weary tree is carried out. At our house the children ate the apples taken off the tree. At other homes (without children) special big candies wrapped in foil with a picture on top and fringes at each end came down, and as guests, we got to eat one each. After the refreshments, we went home contented. At night in our beds we would think sadly of how far away the next Christmas was.

LASKIAINEN — SHROVETIDE

There are many special days marked in red in the *Almanac*, such as *Kynttilän päivä* or Candle Day in February that used to mean something to folks older than I. It somehow measures time as you hopefully look for the coming of spring. February 9th is *Laskiainen* or Shrovetide, which to all the children means a day for sledding and sleigh rides on the snow covered fields and hills. The snow carries you in February because the sun warms the snow during the day, yet at night, a hard crust freezes on the top of the snow. You won't sink in February snow! There are usually special Shrovetide buns waiting for you as you return home from your sledding. They are somewhat like hot cross buns — with delicious fillings.

Traditional Food for the Season

Laskiainen, which means the descent into Lent, is a time of outdoor fun: downhill skiing, sledding, sliding down on *pulkkas* or on a piece of cardboard. I am sure there are horse-pulled sleigh rides too. In northern Minnesota, Finnish Americans gather at the schoolhouse in Palo for craft demonstrations, food, and outdoor fun.

Laskiainen happens just before Ash Wednesday. For example, in 1998, *Laskiais* Sunday was on the 22nd of February and the *Laskiais* Tuesday, the day before Ash Wednesday. Along with the religious season of *Laskiainen*, the weather season is when the sun melts the surface of the snow, which freezes at night, thus making it easy to walk, ski, or go sledding on the crust that can support even a horse and a sleigh full of people.

As teenagers, we went sledding on cardboards at night

where there was light. After dragging our cardboards up the hills, down we came alone or in bunches.

When we got home from the sledding, Mother sometimes had *laskiaispullat* for us — delicious buns filled with a mixture of butter, cream, and almonds, so rich they melt on your tongue.

Laskiaispullat or **Lenten Buns**

Dough:
1/2 *pulla* dough recipe
1   egg beaten with a little
       sugar for glaze
Filling:
1   cup sugar
1/2 cup butter
1   cup whipped cream
1   cup almonds, ground
Confectioner's sugar

Grease the cookie sheets. Shape the already risen *pulla* dough into small balls, about 1/2 cup each. Let rise about 15 minutes in a warm place. Before baking, brush with egg glaze and sprinkle with confectioner's sugar. Bake at 400° for about 15 minutes.

Filling: Cream the butter and sugar until smooth. Add almonds and mix well. In another bowl, whip the cream until it's fluffy.

When the buns have cooled, slice off the top, about 1/2 inch, and save. Remove just a small amount of the inside of bun and fill the cavity with about 1 tablespoonful of the filling. Top with a dab of whipped cream. Replace the "cap," and dust with confectioner's sugar. Makes about 36 buns. It's a treat!

KALEVALA DAY

    The Finnish epic poem, the *Kalevala,* is about life: creation, beauty, challenge, love, hate, death. It is oral poetry that can be sung. SINGING is a power, a weapon of heroes. Enchantment and magic run through the story.

    Elias Lönnrot, physician and poet, collected the material in the *Kalevala* from the people of eastern Finland. When first published in 1835, it created a sensation not only in Finland but abroad. It was acclaimed to be comparable to the masterpieces of western literature. In Finland, it stirred national pride and inspired many artists in different fields.

    The 28th of February is "*Kalevala* Day" with celebrations all over the country in honor of the national epic that inspired Finns and Finnish artists to appreciate the Finnish language, as well as Finnish heritage. There are concerts, poetry recitals, singing and plays performed in schools and theaters. "Welcome here, our grandest guest, / to the joy of our festive moment, / in honor of our great day!" says a *Kalevala* welcoming song.

EASTER

Four Sundays are marked for Lent in February/March. Two Sundays after that is Palm Sunday followed by Maundy Thursday, when Jesus suffered in the hands of his captors. Good Friday and Easter follow.

Easter season brings the oldest of church holidays and many traditions. Easter is celebrated on the Sunday following the moon after the Vernal Equinox. The Finnish word for Easter, *pääsiäinen,* means "getting out" — away from Lent and the winter. On Maundy Thursday a thorough cleaning takes place in homes. The most dreadful time of the year was over at Easter, yet the storehouses were almost empty. Many predictions were based on the Easter morning sunrise. In the early days, people wanted to see the sun "dance" which would mean a good year for the crops and the berries. Even today people go out Easter morning to see the sun rise.

The Easter seasons that hold the best memories were those before I was ten years old; these are of snow and sunshine, pussy willows and magical Easter switches that we made with Y-shaped willow branches and decorated with crepe paper flowers. We'd ski to where the pussy willows grew and bring bunches of them home for the vase. We cut petals and curled their edges with knitting needles, making six flowers, which we attached with thin wire on the upper part of the Y. While working, we were thinking about who would get the switch on Palm Sunday. You most likely chose someone you could count on for a reward! I usually gave mine to my bachelor uncle. On Palm Sunday morning, you knocked on the door of the chosen person, greeted him and asked if he wanted to be touched with this *virpomavihta*. As the answer always was positive, you started touching his body with your magic branch, saying:

> "I touch you with my magic branch
> That will refresh you and keep you well.
> You get the branch, I get a reward."
> *"Virvon, varvon tuoreeks, terveeks,
> Sinulle vihta, minulle lahja."*

On Easter morning you went for your reward, which usually was a chocolate egg with a beautiful ring inside. Today this eastern Karelian tradition has spread over southern Finland, and witches on brooms and copper coffee pots have been added! There were Easter witches and trolls in the old tales; today the witches are good and apparently like to drink coffee — that's why the coffee pots.

A special Easter dish is called "mämmi," which is a dark brown cereal-type food made of sweetened malts. It is baked in the oven and served in birch bark dishes. It is eaten with cream and sugar, and is most delicious.

Traditional Food for the Season

Easter — *Mämmi*

Mämmi *is served at Easter as a dessert.* Traditionally it was baked in a birch-bark basket, but since the use of birch-bark is prohibited to prevent damage to trees in Finland, cardboard baskets (boxes) or other baking dishes are used. This recipe is one used by Sinikka Garcia's mother.

3 qts. water
1 lb. rye malt*
1 1/2 lbs. rye flour
1/4 tsp. salt
1 Tbsp. orange peel

*Malt is grain soaked in water until it sprouts, and is then dried and aged.

Bring water to a bubbling boil and stir in 1/4 lb. of the malt. Move pot to a warm place and add a layer of rye flour on top. Cover and let stand for about 2 hours.

Mix the mixture (pudding) well and add another layer of rye flour and malt on top. Again place the pot in a warm place for 1 hour. Repeat the process hourly until all the malt and rye flour have been used.

Finally, bring mixture to a boil, stirring constantly, and add salt and orange peel. Boil for about 10 minutes, continuing to stir.

Pour *mämmi* into baking dishes, filling just 3/4 full since it expands in the baking. Bake for 3 hours at 200°.

Serve cold with cream or milk and sugar. It's a delicious, earthy taste and should be savored slowly.

To add to this special treat at Easter time, decorate the table with pussy willows and daffodils in a vase.

VAPPU — MAY DAY

Before *Vappu* there are a few special days noted in the Almanac: Finnish Language Day honors Mikael Agricola who wrote the Finnish ABC Book and translated the New Testament into Finnish, and there is Veterans' Day, a patriotic event.

Vappu happens on the first of May, and encourages memories of many things to many people. I remember the parades with all kinds of red flags and brass bands. That was in honor of national Labor Day. I remember the pompons and helium balloons, summer shoes and wearing my thin spring coat — no matter how cold it was — to celebrate the coming of summer!

Perhaps the most interesting part is for students who graduate after passing difficult comprehensive tests in language, mathematics, history, and writing. In Helsinki they celebrate at the Havis Amanda Fountain at South Harbor, wearing their caps of white velvet with a black rim and a golden lyre. They sing and cheer as they place a cap also on Havis Amanda, the nude, gracious maiden of the fountain. Holding armfuls of flowers given to them by their families and friends, they form a parade through the streets to the tomb of the unknown soldier. They sing and lay their flowers there.

There are tasty treats for this holiday: *sima,* a yeast-fermented homemade drink that bubbles, tickling your nose. You eat *tippaleipä* with it, which is a deep-fried tangle of doughnut dough, dusted with powdered sugar. Simply delicious!

The celebration continues all night, and *sima* often is replaced by intoxicating drinks.

There are many special days, especially in the first six months of the year. After *Vappu* comes *Helatorstai* or Ascension Day and *Helluntai* or Whitsuntide on the 18th of May. The song about it says, "It is *Helluntai,* a summer Sunday .... It is the time of song and enjoyment," however, the word *Helluntai* means Pentecostal and people of that religion are called *helluntailaisia.*

Traditional Food and Drink

May Day *Sima*

Sima is a refreshing, tangy, bubbly lemon drink of Finland made especially for May Day, or simply a summer treat. The bubbles result from a dab of yeast added to the cooling brew.

4 qts. water	2 lemons, peeled and sliced
1 1/2 cups granulated sugar	Peel of the 2 lemons
1 cup brown sugar	1/8 tsp. active dry yeast
	1 Tbsp. raisins

Heat water to boiling and stir in sugars. Peel lemons, removing the white layer under the skin. Add lemon slices and peel to the hot water-sugar mixture. Cool to lukewarm. Add the yeast and stir lightly. Let the covered mixture stand overnight (8-10 hours) in a warm place. Tiny bubbles appear when the delicious flavor is reached. Strain the liquid and pour into sterile bottles. Add a pinch of sugar and a few raisins to each bottle. Cork tightly. Let stand at room temperature until the raisins rise to the top. Store in refrigerator, otherwise fermentation continues and flavor is lost. *Sima* should not taste of yeast.

Sima is often accompanied by scrumptious *tippaleivät*.

Tippaleivät — Drop Bread

2 eggs	1/2 tsp. salt
1 1/2 tsp. sugar	2 cups flour
1/2 pkg. active dry yeast	Cooking oil for
2 Tbsp. warm water	deep frying
1 cup milk	Confectioner's sugar

Beat the eggs and sugar lightly. Dissolve the yeast in water and mix with the milk. Stir in the salt and flour. Put in a warm place to rise until bubbly, about 45 minutes.

In a heavy pan, heat the oil (4 inches deep) to about 375°. Cut off a corner of a plastic bag (about 1/8 inch). Put a cupful of batter into the bag. Squeeze batter through the hole into the hot oil, moving the bag in a circular motion until a tangle resembling a bird's nest appears (about 3 inches in diameter). Fry for about a minute, turning the "drop bread" over. Remove and drain on a paper towel. When cooled, sprinkle with confectioner's sugar. These *tippaleivät* are scrumptious when eaten right away or later when they become crisp. Enjoy!

MOTHER'S DAY

Äidille
To My Mother on Mother's Day 1975

Wood anemones I'd bring you,
Set the table, the coffee brew.
"Dear Mother, so many nights you…"
Bravely again I'd sing to you.

All occasions in my country
tie with the nature of my land;
May 1st, Whitsun and Midsummer
bring deep longing to my heart.

On the wings of imagination,
White anemones to you I'd send.
May good fortune be your companion,
May contentment be your guest.

— Sinikka Grönberg Garcia

Perhaps universally, the second Sunday in May is for mothers. My memories are of the time in Helsinki when I was twelve or thirteen. The sunlight is special around Mother's Day; the double windows have been taken down, and the single windows let in more light and sound. The nights are lighter and shorter. The air is crisp; nature is waking from winter's hold. The snow has mostly vanished, and it is time for white anemones and the rare blue ones. They grow in the woods in green and white hummocks under the leafless trees.

The evening before Mother's Day, my sister and I would go into the woods to pick a bouquet, and place it on the kitchen table after Mother had retired. We set the table, and the next morning made coffee. When Mother and everyone came to the kitchen, we shyly sang a song thanking Mother for the sleepless nights we may have caused, and for all her work and caring.

JUHANNUS — MIDSUMMER

On the Saturday between June 20th and 26th, Finns celebrate Midsummer Day *(Juhannus),* the longest day of the year. In the word *Juhannus* is "John," St. John. *Juhannus* honors St. John the Baptist, and is Finland's Flag Day. The Finnish flag flies throughout the nightless night only at this time. The ways of celebrating *Juhannus* vary, depending upon where you are, but there are many traditional ways.

One wants to be near water — a lake or an ocean. It is an outdoor festival — among fragrant birches; an idyllic setting for a festival that celebrates the high point of summer. There is a bonfire by the water — for dreaming — a band playing dance music, and a platform for dancing. There is an uplifting speech delivered among the fragrant birches. There's a romantic summer poem, a chorus and the audience singing, *"Mä oksalla ylimmällä..."* or "I'm standing on top of the tallest tree, seeing shimmering bands of lakes. If I were a gallant eagle, I'd rise up to God in heaven...Let our lakes shimmer with our love, and give us the fervor to always love our country..."

There's food and drink and people old and young; families all out together, and lovers out alone. There is folkdancing; there are games; there's a play, perhaps, and singing and invigorating music! The *Juhannus* night is magic beyond description with its lightness, its colors, its white *Juhannus* roses and the fragrance of lilies of the valley and lilacs. The white and blue flag is waving against the sky atop the birches, reminding you of the sweetness, the struggles for independence, and those who gave their lives. The mystery of the *Juhannus* night also excites the tradition of maidens picking seven kinds of flowers in order to see their future lover's reflection in the well. Everyone wants to be with someone at *Juhannus,* to watch the flames — the dreams — of the bonfire dance against the blue of the sky.

The birch tree is a symbol of *Juhannus.* Birch trees frame the main doorways of many homes. Birch branches and symbols of the birch tree are also seen on city buses, store fronts, and church altars. I have never forgotten the lilacs in bloom for *Juhannus.* Their time is short-lived like *Juhannus* itself.

A special *Juhannus* treat, when we were children, was a crate of soda pop our father brought home. Only at *Juhannus* could you have enough soda! Red raspberry was my favorite kind; it painted my lips red.

The *Juhannus* festivities were held at the sports center in my hometown, but when living in Helsinki, we took a boat to an island where festivities were held. We camped there without sufficient equipment against the cold of the night or the mosquitoes. The early morning hours were miserable!

There are more weddings during *Juhannus* time than at any other time of the year. The spirit of renewal and celebration makes the event even more wonderful — the beauty of the young couple in their wedding attire, the wedding ceremony with its blessing, then the hugs and kisses, the rice, the gifts, and the wedding waltz. One lucky girl catches the bouquet of lilies of the valley, and the dream goes on.

American Finns celebrate *Juhannus,* too. It is their second most important celebration of the year — after Christmas. There's song and dance to the *humppa* and polka. There is no *Juhannus* without a Finnish-American poet's poem. At Finn Halls they usually have a play for all to see. There's food and drink and good company. The smoke coming out of the sauna chimney means the sauna will be ready for the renewal ritual, and the lake or pool is waiting to cool you off. There is always good company.

You will find everything in the Finnish-American *Juhannus* except — at least for me — the mystique of the *Juhannus* night itself. Perhaps the dark of Arizona *Juhannus* nights I've experienced for over forty years has made it impossible for me to find it.

ST. URHO'S DAY

The Truth About St. Urho

St. Urho's Day is an invention of Finnish Americans, who the Irish say were envious of their annual St. Patrick's celebration on the 17th of March. So the Finnish Americans began celebrating their saint's day on March 16, a day before the Irish!

There are a number of claims about the invention of St. Urho lore which bear exploration. After considerable research, as all saints merit, trails lead to Virginia, Minnesota, on the Iron Range. In 1953, Richard Mattson, then a manager at Ketola's department store in Virginia, was pressed to respond when one of his co-workers chided him "that the Finns did not have saints like Saint Patrick." He quickly fabricated a story, thinking…St. Eero, St. Jussi, St. Urho…St. Urho seemed more commanding, so he said, "We have St. Urho. To save the grape crop, he drove the poisonous frogs from Finland before the last ice age." As the legend grew, a professor of psychology, Sulo Havumaki, in 1958 at Bemidji State, changed St. Urho's history from frogs to grasshoppers. And it has been grasshoppers ever since.

Further invention of St. Urho lore has been attributed to two men from New York Mills, Minnesota: Hugh Millin and Einar Saarela, who might have gotten the idea from Professor Havumäki.

Menahga and Finland, Minnesota, each host St. Urho festivals. Both have erected statues of St. Urho; that of Finland's resembles a twenty-two foot high totem pole; Menahga's statue shows St. Urho standing tall at sixteen feet, rivaling Paul Bunyan.

Another rumor has it that the idea came from Toivo O'Flaherty — a half Finn who spread the word among the Irish at bars in Bemidji by telling of the similarity between the natives of Finland and the Floodwood's people. According to him they talked the same, ate the same, wore the same clothes, and differed only in that the Finns paid their war reparations, and the Floodwood people did not. O'Flaherty remarked also that there were no grasshoppers in Finland because St. Urho sent them away — according to his guru Rasputin Mäki. Overhearing this, the Finns got busy with the celebration of their own St. Urho.

So, it is claimed that St. Urho got rid of the grasshoppers in Finland to save the vineyards from the chomping pre-locustidae with a pitchfork and by casting a spell that says:

> *"Heinäsirkka, heinäsirkka,*
> *Mene täältä hiiteen!"*

translated:

> "Grasshopper, grasshopper,
> Get away from here!"

Actually, *hiiteen* refers to "hell," but the corresponding word in Finnish is not the common word for the place, but a much more poetic and acceptable one; perhaps "underworld."

Joseph Kyllönen is credited with working for seven years to get all fifty governors of the U.S.A. to proclaim St. Urho's Day a national holiday. Minnesota Governor Wendell A. Anderson was the first do so in 1975. The proclamations are all framed and displayed at the North Dakota Finnish-American Historical Society in Brockett.

Urho Day is celebrated with parades and festivities everywhere that there are Finnish Americans. The official celebrating started in Minnesota in 1976, and in Butte, Montana — where the Finns are the second largest ethnic group after the Irish —

a representative of St. Urho has appeared since 1985 in the annual parade, riding in his chariot dressed in green and purple attire, his Viking helmet on his head, his pitchfork displayed piercing a giant pre-locustidae.

Now, as to the issue of St. Urho's burial place, Hugh Mellin decided that he had to be buried in Finn Creek, a Finnish-American Open Air Museum in New York Mills, Minnesota. When Wesley E. Sebeka, a rock collector, brought Hugh a slab of rock he had found, Hugh immediately saw St. Urho's face on it and was convinced the saint was buried in Finn Creek.

Learning that saints are always buried thirty feet under, Hugh started doubting that it could be true in this case. Finn Creek was very active; it ran high all year. How could anybody be buried under it? His research produced the answer; a legend showed that the summer St. Urho died was so dry that Finn Creek ran only three days a week! Obviously, St. Urho must have been buried on one of those dry days!

In Helsinki, Richard Mattson, the saint's creator, found St. Urho's Pub, which has silhouettes of "fellow" monks in the windows. Some Finnish Americans tend to favor the opinion of Tauri Aaltio, the ex-director of the Finland Society, who is quoted as saying, "St. Urho is a joke that ran away!" In Finnish: "St. Urho *on karkuunpäässyt leikinlasku."* Perhaps it doesn't really matter! Who knows where and when miracles begin and end?

Celebrate with Special Foods

St. Urho's Day Rye Bread
From *Fantastically Finnish*

1 1/2 cups dark beer
1/2 cup milk
2 1/2 cups dark rye or pumpernickel rye flour
1 cup cracked wheat
2 tsps. salt
1 tsp. crushed anise seed
2 tsps. crushed fennel seed
1 Tbsp. grated orange peel
2 pkgs. active dry yeast
1/4 cup warm water
1 Tbsp. dark corn syrup
2-2 1/2 cups bread flour

In a saucepan, heat beer and milk to a boil (milk will curdle). Measure rye flour and cracked wheat into large bowl and add boiling mixture. Stir in salt, anise, fennel and orange peel. Let cool to about 105°. In a small bowl, dissolve yeast in the warm water and add the corn syrup, let stand until foamy, about 5 minutes; stir into cooled mixture. Add bread flour gradually to make a stiff dough. Let stand 15 minutes.

Turn out onto lightly floured board and knead for 10 minutes until dough is smooth and springy. Wash bowl, grease it, and put dough into bowl. Turn dough over to grease top; cover and let rise until doubled, about 1 1/2 to 2 hours. Punch down. Turn out onto lightly oiled surface and shape into a smooth round loaf. Cover a baking sheet with parchment paper or lightly grease it. Place loaf on baking sheet with smooth side up. Let rise again until almost double, about 45 minutes to 1 hour. Slash top with a sharp knife in three parallel cuts going each way on the loaf, making 1-inch squares. Bake in preheated 375° oven for 40-45 minutes, or until loaf sounds hollow when tapped. Makes 1 large loaf.

St. Urho's Day Fish Stew
from *Fantastically Finnish*

6	large potatoes, pared, cut into chunks	3	lbs. cleaned freshwater fish (i.e. trout, walleye, whitefish)
1	large onion, diced	2	cups heavy cream or 1 can evaporated milk
2	tsps. salt		
5	whole allspice	2	Tbsp. butter
6	cups water		Dill weed to taste

In a large soup kettle, put potatoes, onion, salt, allspice and water. Cover and bring to a boil. Simmer 15 to 20 minutes until potatoes are tender. Cut fish into 2-inch chunks. Lower fish into the pot, cover and simmer 15 minutes until fish flakes when probed with a fork.

Stew should not boil; fish should remain in rather large pieces. (If overcooked, it falls apart.)

Add cream, butter and dill weed if desired. Serve hot. Makes 6 servings.

Customs

AT A MEMORIAL SERVICE

In 1997, I attended the memorial service for my mother in Finland. I was impressed with the dignity of the Finnish custom of remembering friends and relatives. It was a very moving occasion, starting with the tolling of the "death bells" from the chapel steeple — a slow, haunting sound carrying far. A memorial service in Finland is a solemn happening, not as much a celebration of life as it often is here in America. People express their sorrow for the loss of a dear one through tears and religious faith in verse and song. During our memorial service, each family group or individual presented a flower arrangement at the coffin on the catafalque, reading out the verse of their choice as they took their proper place in front. The grandchildren and the great grandchildren each placed a rose on their *Mummo's* coffin. People still dress in somber black or black and white, to show sorrow for their loss and respect for the deceased. They pour out their praise and their hope in hymns such as this:

Spiritual 631, translated by S. G.

"O Lord, let this wanderer of the earth
at the end of my journey
see You, Lord, in your glory.

"Do let me in with the blessed
to be with my kin and friends.
Please let me in to be
with the Lord of mercy!"

Hymn 341, translated by S. G.

"I praise you God
for all the mercy
shown to me during my life.
I thank you for the splendid
spring days and for the
gloomy days of fall.

"Thank you, Lord,
for every moment.
Thank you for the battles fought.
Thank you for the cross also.
Thank you for your help in pain.

"Thank you Lord, for all the flowers
that bloomed so nicely on my way.
Thank you also for the thistles
that hurt my feet as I went on.
Thank you for the promise of
life eternal; for everything
I thank you, Lord!"

The verse attached to my family's flowers was from my favorite poem "Birds" by Uuno Kailas, a beloved Finnish poet.

"...Life is beautiful. Therefore sing!
Death is long. Therefore sing!
Weave sunset, clouds, dew, happiness
into your sweetest melodies.

> "As you awoke, the wing of a lullaby
> touched your head.
> The same way you'll fall asleep.
> Over your tomb, the bird
> of balance will fly with wings unseen."
>
> Translated by S. G.

Death announcements in Finnish newspapers take up a large section. They are about three-by-three inches each, and in addition to the facts about the deceased and the names of the bereaved, a poem is included. Ours said:

> "What is that love that
> lasts all life 'til death,
> asking for nothing,
> yet giving everything.
> Taking care, guiding.
> There's only one kind;
> it's called Mother's love."

At the parish hall, a Karelian style dinner was served. The tears had been wiped away for the moment, and there was a happy meeting of cousins and cozy chatter among friends. The minister, who knew Mother, spoke of her as being well-liked and needed by many. My brother Pentti spoke about Mother's work and determination, to which I added the following story:

It was November 1939 when Mother, my brother Juhani, six; my sister Anja, three, and I, eight, were on the train with hundreds of other evacuees — women and children — heading west (via south) from Värtsilä, Eastern Finland, away from the war the Russians had started. It was a dark, starless night when the call came to evacuate, and masses of muted women and children with their belongings filled the road to the train station.

Farewells had been said; the train was dimly lit; the Army

nurses were serving milk and hardtack sandwiches to the children. Soon there was peace on board, but suddenly we awoke to the command, "Get out, jump into the snowdrift!" Enemy planes were above. Dark trains in a white snow field were good targets for bombing. This happened twice that night before we came to another station where we transferred to another train. There was no bombing. What madness it was trying to keep up with Mother while dragging the big bag of belongings behind me in the throng of people! Mother took care of my sister and brother and a big suitcase. As the oldest, I had to manage somehow on my own.

Mother conceived a plan: she sought out two military officers, asking them where their train was going to go. "West," they said. "Please take me and my children with you!" begged Mother. After a while, they agreed to let us board. The comfort of the officers' compartment in their train was wonderful, and we reached our destination at Massilanmäki, in the province of Savo, without difficulty. All was well until the next morning's news, "Evacuee Train Bombed: Casualties High." The enemy had bombed the civilian train which we were supposed to have been on going north. Mother had changed our destiny. I told the gathering at the parish hall about my son Tom who, upon hearing this, realized the significance of Mother's (his *Mummo's*) courageous decision — he might not even exist today!

The north wind was blowing hard as we left the parish hall, making us hurry along. In crunchy snow, following deep footsteps, we walked to our father's grave, covered with Mother's flowers and surrounded by snow in the winter evening's pale glow. Mother's ashes would be laid to rest there in a few days. I would be gone, but my immediate family would hold another memorial service with candles and flowers then.

NIMIPÄIVÄ — NAME DAY

The University of Helsinki's *Almanac* places over seven-hundred men's and women's names on its pages for each month of the year. Every person has a Name Day in the *Almanac*. For most dates, there are several names. The names on each date are derived from the same root, such as "Anja, Anita, Anniina, Anitta" on October 22nd. My name, Sinikka, has its day on the second of September. This tradition may come from the old Roman saints' names found in the Catholic almanacs.

Having a Name Day is a joy because your age is not relevant. There are thousands of celebrants by the same name at the same time! The most common name days are known by heart and are easily remembered by most people. Friends show up at your door with a bouquet of flowers, a pack of coffee or just send a message to wish you happiness. Fax and electronic-mail help out today, but flowers are still very much in style for both men and women. In 1949 on September 2nd, I received four bouquets from four different boyfriends! They came to our cabin; one stayed, the others just handed me their flowers and congratulations, then left on their bicycles.

Flowers play an important role in Finland. At graduation time, boys, as well as girls, receive armfuls of flowers from their family and friends. Flowers are pictured in portraits. Whenever you go for a visit, even if it is not a special celebration, you may pick up a bouquet. Flower sellers are abundant at street corners all over town in the summer. In the winter you stop by a florist shop or pick up your flowers at the railway station in the heart of Helsinki.

There are complaints about the expense of the flower tradition, but it endures. A friend, who lived on a pension, added up the money she had spent on flowers in one year — 1,000 marks or about $200. Flowers bring cheer, especially in the dark months. Tulips are preferred in winter. In place of wreathes, great arrangements of roses, azaleas, iris, lilacs, and even orchids are used. A stem of twelve orchids arrived at my sister's home as a condolence after Mother's death.

Children's birthdays are celebrated much the same in Finland as they are in the U.S.A., with invitations, cake and candles, decorations, gifts, games and the birthday song. Often the song is the Finnish version of "Happy birthday to you...," but in some families in Finland there is a traditional congratulatory song sung for both birthdays and name days. Guests sing as they enter and everyone joins in. For one recent birthday, my brother and his wife sang the song to me over a cellular phone as they were fighting the traffic on their way to work.

For adults, only birthdays ending in a zero are celebrated in a big way with a buffet, flowers, gifts and singing, and maybe dancing. Of course, you may do whatever you choose on your special day.

A SUMMER WEDDING

In Finland, summer weddings are special because nature is at its best, and people seem happier. Under blissful sunshine and a cloudless sky, most of the celebrating happens outdoors on the lawn or in the garden surrounded by trees and flowers.

The wedding ceremony is held most likely in a small country church built of stone or wood and painted white or red. Anything old-fashioned is considered uplifting and respectful. The ceremony itself is not unlike wedding ceremonies anywhere else. There are the beautiful bride and groom walking elegantly down the aisle in a church decorated with flowers, the guests dressed in their best, the organ music, the minister's prayers and blessings, the vows and the ring exchange, and the kiss. Instead of the strains of "Here comes the bride," the couple may walk to the majestic music of the "Festival March" by Kuula, a Finnish composer. The guests listen to the minister, pray, sing and rejoice.

At the end of the ceremony, grand organ music leads the newlyweds out of the church, and the guests follow. At the top of the tall stairs leading down from the church, the newlyweds are showered with rice; the bridal bouquet, usually lilies-of-the-valley, is thrown. Cameras flash, and a line of cars forms a caravan to drive to the party, where the white and blue Finnish flag is waving, adding a festive feeling to the moment. An honor guard is formed along the path leading to the lawn, and the wedding party is cheered and welcomed as it walks through.

Blue-and-white striped tents are set up for the dinner; guests are ranked and seated according to their relationship to the newly married. Time is spent becoming acquainted with the new family and reinstating old ties. The menu is roast beef and lamb, delicious tiny potatoes, fruits and vegetables and garnished dishes of many kinds. There is champagne for toasting, and beer and wine, along with delicious homemade strawberry cakes. People are happy; the children play.

Then there are the surprises! At one point, for instance, the bride and the groom appear on the lawn outside the tents. The bride sits down, the groom remains standing. A group of young men — the Singers — approach and sing a romantic song to the bride. Then they pick her up and steal her away! To get her back, the groom has to give a speech; he has to keep talking until someone decides it is enough. At times when he runs out of topics to talk about, the groom gets help from his father. At one particular wedding, the groom told the guests that he was going to help the Singers with their song because it was difficult to understand. The difficult song turned out to have only one word: "Amen!" But it was sung in such enchanting harmony and repeated in so many rounds that it left the audience in awe. When the Singers reappeared with the bride, there was much hilarity, and applause.

Several hours into the party, at midnight, two men appear dressed as doctors, carrying carving instruments. They lead the people into the darkened woods, where a "robber's roast" is found buried in a pit. As the pit is uncovered, there is a delicious smell of steaming meat. The meat is cut up and served rustically on a slice of birch tree trunk. There is much toasting, and the Singers sing. There are speeches and more drinks for toasting as many huddle around the warmth of the pit.

The band plays for hours, and the dance floor fills again. By three a.m., most of the people have gone home, but some stay behind to visit. The newlyweds have long since left for their honeymoon on the sea, in a sailboat, sailing toward the rising sun somewhere on the Gulf of Finland.

TALKOOT — "WORKING BEES"

In the olden days when your house construction reached the point where the ridge pole was ready to be raised, a celebration was called for, as were food, drinks and speeches. The work was always done with volunteers who worked under the supervision of the builder. This voluntary teamwork, *talkoot* ("working bees"), was still a widely spread tradition in the 50s and 60s.

Our family home near Helsinki was built that way in 1951. On the first weekend, we helped pour the foundation, and on the second weekend, with the help of fourteen friends and neighbors the chimney was constructed. Brick brigades were formed; concrete was mixed in a man-powered mixer which we took turns tumbling. The mix was wheeled in a wheelbarrow, and the bricks passed to two brick masons, whose position kept changing as the chimney grew in height. The entire chimney was completed from the three-meter deep basement up through two stories, the attic and the roof.

In spite of the hard work, the spirit was superb. Throughout the day, there was fun and laughter; there were coffee breaks and meal times for chatting. At the end of the day, everyone stretched out aching backs, groaning and moaning, then hurried to have a sauna bath at one of the neighbors. Sleep came without coaxing, in the attics of neighbors, after the ever-sweet healing touch of the sauna.

In return, such work had to be reciprocated because there were many houses going up at the same time! The lots were issued to war veterans and to the Karelians like us who had lost our piece of land to the Russians at Lake Jänisjärvi in 1940.

On the farms after a "bee" of haying in the summer heat, a sauna was enjoyed before getting ready for a barn dance, where polkas, tangos, schottisches, mazurkas, and waltzes were danced till the morning hours.

Times changed and much of the "bee" work seemed to have gone away with the changes, but currently, since the 70s and 80s, a village movement has been at work to restore volunteerism in rural areas. The aim is to stem migration from the villages to cities by making the villages more attractive, socially and economically rewarding, and cozy places to live, as well as to persuade people to move in, and to create means of livelihood. This grassroots movement started in the most remote villages as a counterattack to save the impoverished villages that had lost their people to the cities where labor was in demand and a modern and fashionable lifestyle was advertised. The approach is different in different places, but one common condition is a lack of funds with an abundance of skillful and motivated people, whose "secret weapon" is the voluntary teamwork — *talkoot* ("working bees"). Millions of hours of work have been donated for the common good — work substituting for money and rewarding pleasure that is derived from working together. It is a strong basis for good human relations, and it creates a feeling of mutual belonging among the people living in the same village.

The restoration of buildings — for instance workshops where the women do weaving — is happening. Roads are improved, ball parks, boat harbors, jogging and skiing tracks, and swimming places at the lakes are being constructed. Many cellars have been converted into motor and car repair shops. Senior citizens are being taken care of better than before, and schools are being reopened.

Local traditions are being restored in the form of celebrations, compiling histories, handicrafts, renovation of buildings and homes, and establishing local museums and exhibitions. Amateur theaters are thriving! A need to draw from heritage and history is evidenced in this re-building of self-image. Cultural events, such as fairs, festivals, theater, concerts and song fests, draw visitors and bring to fruition the work done by so many.

According to experts, there is no doubt that the village movement strengthens the social structure in Finland. As long as people can work together, they'll be able to maintain meaningful and dignified lives regardless of the amount of money available.

THE SAUNA

Perhaps the most universally known Finnish tradition is the SAUNA, which is pronounced "sowna" (as in female pig) not "sawna." The idea for the sauna is not new, nor was it invented by the Finns. Many European nations had a similar bathing ritual in the past; the Greeks, Romans, and the Turks are known for them. Even today, in rural Mexico, steam baths called *temascal* are used. These are heated from the outside, and you crawl into them. The American-Indian sweat houses are for medicinal cleansing, not for weekly bathing.

The Finnish sauna has a long history that has stayed with the Finns. The farm people used to build the sauna first — living in it while building their dwelling. Many functions, such as giving birth and bloodletting ("cupping") were performed in the sauna well into the twentieth century.

The sauna culture has spread throughout the world. Thousands of saunas are being built in the U.S.A. yearly. In

Finland, a land of slightly over 5,000,000 people, there are millions of saunas near the 100,000 lakes, on sea and island shores, and in homes, condominiums and flats in the cities.

A true sauna has to meet a few requirements. The heater *(kiuas)* must have rocks over the heating unit. The inside of a sauna must be made of wood: the walls (horizontal wall boards), the benches, the washroom, and the dressing room. (This has to do with the smell and the atmosphere; walls made of tile just won't do, except perhaps in the washroom.) The sauna has to be a relaxing, warm place. The lighting is subdued.

They say a wood-burning sauna is best — the heat being sweeter and the smell of burning wood delightful. There is something also to be said about the ritual of heating the sauna with wood and waiting for hours for it to be ready on a Saturday night after a hard week's work. Saunas at weekend retreats by the water usually afford that luxury as people have more time. The lake or seashore also offers a refreshing splash into the water after the sauna. Automatic electric or a gas heaters are used, too, and swimming pools and snow banks may take the place of a lake.

Relaxing both physically and mentally by perspiring — getting cleansed — on the upper bench of the sauna, in dry heat of about 180 degrees Fahrenheit or more, is free of much effort. Your body is having a work-out; the heart speeds up and the capillaries on the surface rush blood to it; your pores open and your skin turns pink and starts to glisten. When you feel like it, you get down and out of the room for a shower or dip in the water. When you go back in, you start throwing dipperfuls of warm water on the hot rocks, thus creating steam that is 15 to 20 percent moisture. The steam does not engulf you the way it does in a Turkish bath where fog forms. At the same time you start touching your skin — slapping legs, arms, back — with a switch of birch leaves (eucalyptus in Tucson, Arizona) that disperse a wonderful aroma that helps you relax more. What a wonderful feeling! You might prefer to be alone, in which case you have a chance to lie down on the bench; or if you prefer to be with someone, the talk is about pleasant things. You add to the heat by throwing more water on the rocks, or you may lower it, or go out for another shower or dip.

In the hot room, you listen and feel with your senses. In the shower room, you talk as you scrub. My family's best times for discussion were in the sauna. It has been said that President Urho Kekkonen used his time in the sauna for preliminary consultations before top level conferences. (Nowadays there are many women ministers, therefore no more sauna sessions!) You scrub someone's back and get the favor returned. In a pay per sauna, you pay for a scrubber, or even for a masseuse. They are always women.

In a sauna you get rid of bad thoughts and anger, as well as mosquito bites, aching muscles and joints. There is nothing sexual about the sauna. (From childhood on, the Finns get used to naked bodies. There is no shame in it.) The sauna babies you! You get physically and mentally refreshed. Your skin feels silky between the sheets of your bed. And afterwards, when you join the company at hand at the big table for soft drinks, coffee and *pulla,* juice or a beer, you feel good about being part of a circle of friends and family.

THE SUMMER COTTAGE SYNDROME

Some say that Finland closes down for the summer. Many businesses used to close for the entire month of July — and some still do — but now many cater to the summer tourist trade. Actually, what is meant by "closing for the summer" is that it is hard to find anybody you want to see in the city during the summer because they have all fled to the country. At the least, they head for their summer places for the weekend. This phenomenon has everything to do with being close to nature: to take a sauna every evening, to swim, to go boating, to get away from it all. What a thrill to be freshly bathed from the sauna and to have "sauna sausage" for dinner with your favorite drink under a birch tree!

At the summer cottage *(kesämökki)*, one lives freely, either with or without neighbors, after a long winter spent mostly indoors. Expanding yourself by wandering in the woods, picking blueberries or sun-ripe wild strawberries in July, and gathering flowers — bluebells, daisies, buttercups — on the meadow is invigorating. One can bathe in the sun, in the lake or sea water, and in the sauna. The glistening bay and its sounds, the sailboats in the distance, the smoke from the sauna chimney, the twitter of birds have a curative effect; one delights in them. One anticipates the sweet cuckoo's call — in spite of ominous associations. With slight apprehension, one listens and counts the calls that will tell how many more years one will live. One knows it isn't so, but…still…

Energy is restored. Being conscious of the fact that the summer is short and that autumn isn't far away, helps motivate storing up for the darkness of November and December. Hard work in preparation for this holiday doesn't matter. At the end of the vacation, everything is hauled back to the city; schools start, and one gets back to a routine — refreshed and ready.

There have been weekend escapes throughout time, but this custom spread to the middle class in the 60s. Today one in five Finns has a summer cottage. How did folks get by without summer cottages or winter vacations on the beaches of southern Europe or on the northern fells or in ski resorts? They had, of course, no traffic or computer problems, only an eternal worry about their daily bread, the weather and the crops, an early frost, or a draught. Perhaps the exhausting physical work earned needed rest, and the familiar tranquil land maintained a person's peace of mind. Leisure time activities have become a new worry for modern man, and the longer life span — a bonus — may be complicating matters. But if a simple summer cottage makes a difference, it is a worthy indulgence to relieve the stresses of modern life!

FINLAND SOCIETY
SUOMI SEURA R.Y.

In 1997 the Finland Society celebrated its 70th Anniversary, along with its magazine *Finland Bridge*. Previously called *Finland Message,* the new name was adopted in 1937.

From the beginning, the purpose of the organization has been to convey news from Finland to expatriates, to inform Finns at home of happenings in the Finnish communities abroad, and to urge Finns abroad to communicate among themselves. Also, the Finland Society defied the negative attitude common at one time among the Finns in Finland toward the Finns who had left their country. The Finland Society, being an interest group and a non-governmental organization, has relayed not only news, but as a natural consequence, has presented proposals and demands. An old truth states, "Strength lies in cooperation and volunteer spirit." This non-profit organization depends on volunteer work and club activities as a basis for its strength.

I became familiar with the Finland Society in 1965 when my children and I traveled to Finland for the first time on one of the society's group flights. We flew on an Icelandic Airlines's propeller aircraft that refueled in Reykjavik. We were ushered onto the plane by Paul Hanslin of Hanslin Travel, and were personally received by Tauri Aaltio, then director of the Finland Society. It was a good feeling not to be just numbers. I believe many Finnish Americans have rediscovered Finland through group flights organized by the Finland Society.

Our local organization, the Finnish-American Club of Tucson, benefited from Tauri Aaltio's personal visit in 1977, and it was beneficial when he nominated me to the "FinnFest" board as a representative of the Southwest. Our club has received books for its library from the society, and a visit by Dr. Martti Häikiö, director after Tauri Aaltio.

At least five members of our Tucson group were present among thousands from abroad at the celebration of "Roots '92" in Helsinki. We set up a booth at the Messuhalli and sold T-shirts, mugs and my new book *The Finn In Me*. I also participated in a meeting at the University of Helsinki with other organizations from abroad. We attended many programs in the city of Helsinki, for instance, *Laulupuun lehtiä,* a poetry recital.

A great contribution of the Finland Society is "FinnFest," which they started in 1982. Time after time at the annual "FinnFest" in the U.S., we renew our ties to the Finland Society by attending presentations, receiving awards and assistance, and by meeting with new personnel.

Their annual "Finland Seminar of Language and Culture," held in Finland for young descendants, also deserves our appreciation! The Expatriate Parliament's preliminary session in August '97, in connection with the 70th Anniversary of the Finland Society, brought Finns from abroad together to explore ways to approach problems and to find new ways of communication.

The Finland Society is a force for unification and identity among Finns abroad. We give heartfelt thanks for this means to keep in touch with our beloved Finland.

To launch a new century in the year 2000, the Finnish-Canadian Cultural Federation and "FinnFest U.S.A." combine resources to hold a "once in a lifetime" grand fest. "We Welcome the World to Preserve, Inspire and Celebrate Finnish Culture" is scheduled for July, 2000, in Toronto, Ontario, Canada.

FINNFEST

"FinnFest U.S.A." was the brain child of two members of the Finland Society *(Suomi Seura)* in Finland: Osmo Kalliala and Tauri Aaltio. In 1982 they got together to talk about their experiences among the Finns abroad, each having traveled extensively to Finnish communities in the U.S.A., Canada and Australia. They were surprised at the rich and active cultural life in these communities, and at the festivities held annually. They came up with the idea of getting Finnish Americans of all the varied organizations in hundreds of Finnish-American communities together for a big annual festival. The purpose, of course, was to enhance heritage, to share common ideas and problems, and to celebrate common roots.

The first meeting was held with representatives from forty-six organizations, among them: Dr. Ralph Jalkanen, President of Suomi Synod, and Dr. Väinö A. Hoover, President of the Finlandia Foundation. There was a contest to name the event, and "FinnFest U.S.A." won. The rules were laid out; the legalities taken care of.

Robert W. Selvälä, appointed head of the Public Relations

Committee, later became president of "FinnFest U.S.A.", a position he has held for many years. Board members represent various geographical areas.

In the summer of 1983, the first "FinnFest" was held in Minneapolis. Subsequent festivals were held in:

Fitchburg, MA	Duluth, MN
Hancock, MI	Thousand Oaks, CA
San Francisco, CA	De Kalb, IL
Detroit, IL	Portland, OR
Newark, DE	Marquette, MI
Seattle, WA	Minot, ND
Hancock, MI	Gorham, ME
Lake Worth, FL	Seattle, WA

Attendance has varied from about 1,500 to over 10,000 people annually. The program consists of a balanced menu of cultural events: lectures, plays, films, concerts, exhibits, sports, and dance. There is Finnish food, music, and shopping *(tori)*. Visitors and artists from Finland participate as well as Finnish-Americans.

The festivals have become a family affair, where meeting with relatives and friends takes place with a feeling of mutual belonging at the root level. "FinnFest" brings us closer to each other; it helps us remember; it increases our interest, and educates us.

The joy and success, the hard work that goes into making a festival of the Finnish-American caliber takes time and dedication.

On "FinnFest '97"

There were 300 Finnish flags flying high, welcoming us to the fairgrounds in Minot, North Dakota, for the fifteenth annual "FinnFest" in 1997, which was a very well organized and memorable event.

One of the highlights of this "FinnFest" was the play *Seven Brothers* by Aleksis Kivi, performed by the Nurmijärvi (Kivi's birth place) Theater's ten actors. The cast included: the seven typically flaxen-haired, vigorous young men; Venla who was the object of their admiration; Venla's mother, and the narrator, who represented Aleksis Kivi himself. Just seeing the play would have justified going to the "FinnFest." It was so grand, so enjoyable — hearing the Finnish language as spoken by the brothers, the humor in their seriousness, and the energy they emitted. (Professor Richard Impola had translated a guide to viewing, which was helpful.)

Another prize experience was a concert by Veli-Matti Järvenpää, whose band did the warm-up for "The Vees" from Fargo, North Dakota, a local rock-and-roll band. Järvenpää, a tall, lanky youth, was dressed in dark-colored denim pants and jacket. His long, blonde hair hanging from under a dark baseball cap would swing from side to side as if in rhythm with the music. His sentimental, rhythmic Tex-Mex music played on several small accordions makes people not only take notice, but prompted several standing ovations — a Finn playing Tex-Mex music to the American Finns! Accompanied by a drummer, an acoustic and an electric guitar, wherever he goes, he masters the role of a rising Finnish star!

Reverend Giles Ekola's presentation on "Scandinavian-American Perspectives" led to lively discussion with the Finland Society magazine's editor-in-chief, Larserik Häggman, on the importance of the old-time Finnish writers (Runeberg, Topelius, Aho), on Marshall Mannerheim's disagreements, and on THE WAR.

THE FINNISH-AMERICAN CLUB OF TUCSON

Local Club Spirit

The day my youngest sister Tuula ran into a person speaking Finnish at the post office in 1968, another dimension was added to my family's life. Instead of just knowing our neighbors and my colleagues at school, we — my husband Chico and our children Quique, Dina, Lisa and Tom — began to meet Finnish Americans in Tucson. Tuula was visiting us that year.

The Finnish-American Club of Tucson was two years old at the time, and they were having a *Juhannus* party that day at the Veterans of Foreign Wars' Hall, with good eating and much visiting. We felt truly welcome.

The club consisted mostly of Minnesota and Michigan Finnish Americans, who had fled the harsh winters of northern climes and moved to Tucson. Most of them had health problems to contend with, and a history of belonging to big, energetic Finn Hall and Co-op organizations. They had experience in their Finnishness and were often of the opinion that they had already done their share.

Not all, of course, held to that opinion. There were a few enthusiastic leaders and several good cooks and hostesses. They passed on customs that we did not know; many spoke Finglish or Finlisk, a combination of English and old-world Finnish, which wasn't easy to understand at first. The striking fact, at the time, was that they were older. Looking back, I now see that they were not any older than I am at the moment! They had a warm, old-fashioned style in manner and dress. Some of them became surrogate grandparents to our children!

Juhannus 1997

Although we missed many vacationing families, the forty-four members present managed to have a good time at our *Juhannus* party in 1997. Even the temperature was a reasonable 104 degrees; the pool was refreshing and the sauna hot. The week before at "FinnFest," I met Kimmo Wilska, our friend from Radio Finland. Upon hearing of his family's plans to head for Tucson, I invited them to our *Juhannus* party, and they came! We were interested in hearing about Kimmo's work. I learned that you can listen to Radio Finland through the Internet any time of the day at your convenience! No more limited-time listening!

Jouni Wilska, age eleven, obliged us by nicely reciting Lauri Pohjanpää's poem, "At *Juhannus* Time," which tells just about everything that makes up *Juhannus* — the nightless night, the skylark's song, the fragrance of the lilacs, the white snow of the apple trees, and the crackling flames of the *Juhannus* bonfire. We sang many songs from, *"Ol' kaunis kesäilta"* to *"Honkain keskellä,"* before it got dark. We enjoyed the symbolic *kokko* made of five torches whose orange flames reflected in the water against the darkening Arizona sky, and we rejoiced in the vanishing heat of the desert.

Many of us watched the de-commercialized version of the "Good Morning, America" show from Finland, drawing our own conclusions about the wife-carrying and boot-tossing contests and such. We appreciated the pre-filmed parts, such as the piece on the Finnish sauna and the Nokia Company. I guess something is better than nothing, and this show was better than the infamous program on the Finnish tango a few years back.

TRAVELING IN FINLAND

Travelers to Finland still find it an uncluttered and unhurried land. The natural setting is still pristine and lovely. The old villages and towns, with their wooden houses and golden wheat fields, are idyllic; its cities with many cultural events and interesting architecture, are inviting. The archipelago of Turku greets you no matter which way you arrive — by air or boat. The Gulf of Finland glistens around hundreds of islands in the summer. In the winter Finland is surrounded by a white blanket of snow-covered ice dotted with dark spots that are the islands.

There are five regions for the visitor to explore: the Southwest, the lake district, Bothnia, East Finland and Lapland. Each is quite different in landscape and culture. The road network and bus system are excellent and the rail system (fast trains) extends as far as Rovaniemi in the Arctic Circle. An excellent Finnair travel service reaches even further north, to Kittilä, however, the best way to see Finland is by car.

The Finnish Southwest: TURKU

The area around Turku is an ancient settlement through which much trade and cultural exchange came to Finland for centuries. That includes Christianity in the form of the Crusades (1156), which eventually led to the conversion of Finland to Roman Catholicism. The Turku Castle was manned by many foreign, as well as native masters in their time. It holds many reminders and relics for the visitor to see and experience. Turku also has an old medieval cathedral, and the Turku archipelago is a yachtsman's paradise. There are other historic towns, such as Naantali with its chamber music festival held in June, and Rauma with its 14th-century Franciscan monastery and a walking tour of the section of wooden houses that are among the best preserved in all Scandinavia.

Turku was the first capital, and had the first diocese and bishops. It also had the first university in Finland. In a day's drive one can visit seven medieval churches — most built of gray stone — that have been in use since their establishment, some from the 1280s. (See "Touring the Medieval Churches.") The scenery is distinctively Finnish with clusters of forest between the ocean bays and red barns in the middle of golden fields of grain.

Following the 13th-century King's Road (now modern, of course) from Turku toward Helsinki, one passes through the southern coastal areas still populated by Swedish-speaking Finns, who have strong ties to the sea. Models of ships hang from the ceilings of their churches as a reminder of the interdependency of faith and the sea. Many of the towns that were villages have been restored to their earlier beauty — wooden houses painted red or yellow with white trimmings. They inspire a feeling of times past — of peace and harmony, idyllic places with a continuous view to the glistening sea. This region was the heart of the iron works industry that goes back to the 16th century. The town of Fiskars is one of these towns proud of its history; today Fiskars scissors are well known and copied all over the world.

Taking a side road you can visit Sammatti where Elias Lönnrot, compiler of the *Kalevala,* lived, and stop at Hanko to see the regattas compete off the peninsula in the Gulf of Finland. (Sea cruises are available.) This region was ceded to the Soviet Union as part of war reparations. They were to keep it for fifty years, but returned it sooner. For years Finnish trains ran through the "Porkkala Tunnel" — as it was called — their windows were covered with metal shades that were put on and removed at the proper time! Hanko, at the southernmost tip of Finland, is a main harbor, which in years past saw thousands of emigrants off to foreign lands. There are miles and miles of sandy beaches, and a full calendar of activities to enjoy.

Traveling further along King's Road takes you to towns that were inhabited as far back as 8000 years ago. The trip offers the visitor a glimpse into Finnish history and into the diverse cultures that have shaped and created the charm of the region itself. The graveyards found in the southern coastal towns are lovely gardens of flowers and peace, well worth stopping to spend a moment reflecting on life. It quiets you as you review the ancient gravestones. The sight of a sea of white crosses erected for those who gave their young lives in securing their country's freedom in the wars of 1939-1944, is stirring.

Southern Finland: HELSINKI

Helsinki, the capital of the Republic of Finland since 1917 and of the Autonomous Finland for a hundred years before that, has about 700,000 inhabitants. In the heart of the city, the buildings of neoclassical design in Senate Square — the Government Palace, the Cathedral, the University — are by the German architect C.L. Engel. Detailed construction was supervised by Czar Nicholas I himself, giving a Russian flavor to some of the buildings such as Uspenski Cathedral with its "onion towers." In spite of the foreign influences, Helsinki has preserved an outlook inherently Finnish in the style of National Romanticism, as well as Functional and Modern architecture. An example is the magnificent Railway Station with its illuminated green tower, designed around 1902 by the famous Finnish architect Eliel Saarinen. Hvitträsk (White Lake), a unique studio house designed and built by Saarinen and other Finnish architects, Gesellius and Lindgren, is charming in architectural detail and history. There are many examples throughout Finland of the work of Alvar Aalto, a Finnish architect who was discovered after designing the Finnish Pavilions for two World Fairs.

A centerpiece of Helsinki is the oldest museum in Scandinavia devoted to Scandinavian design. Recently renovated, the Museum of Art and Design houses a permanent display chronicling the history of Finnish modern design. Displays defining Finland's Modernist sensibility include works by Alvar Aalto, by Antti Nurmesniemi, textiles by Marimekko, Arabia ceramics, and Iittala glass, to name a few. Other museums and art galleries to note are: the Botanical Garden, the Linnanmäki Amusement Park, the Baltic Herring Market, and the Seurasaari Open Air Museum offering many exhibits and events. The Sibelius Monument, located in Sibelius Park, is a dramatic presentation in honor of this beloved composer. There are tours and cruises on land and water, and a variety of performances, especially during Helsinki Week, in theaters, at the Opera House, and at churches (one of special note is Temppelinaukion Kirkko, a church carved from solid rock).

Helsinki has accommodations to suit everyone's taste and pocketbook. Shopping is plentiful, ranging from department stores to flea markets. The South Harbor market is quite famous. You can view the huge ferries docked there, and buy fish directly from the fishermen in their boats. Salmon and other fish are abundant. Home-grown fruits and vegetables, berries, mushrooms, handicrafts, and flowers, as well as sauna switches are for sale.

The Finnish rye bread is out-of-this-world, as are the tiny potatoes and the little-finger-sized hot dogs with hot mustard that are sold on the streets for snacks. Finns eat a lot of cheese, cucumbers and tomatoes, and fresh dill is a favored taste. They drink a lot of coffee, milk, and buttermilk. Homemade Finnish *viili* (yogurt) is great, too. Finnish Finlandia vodka can be bought almost everywhere in the world.

You can travel from Hanko to Helsinki, also, by old steamers revived for excursions, through what is known as the National Archipelago Park. You also can travel by boat from Helsinki to Porvoo, another picturesque old town with interesting remnants from the days of the Russian Empire, located about thirty miles east of Helsinki. Porvoo hosts festivals and exhibits throughout the year.

As school children, we went there to see the tombs of some Finnish heroes, for instance, that of Eugene Schauman, who killed Bobrikov, the notorious Russian governor general, just before the Bolshevik Revolution in Russia and the resulting independence of Finland.

Lakeland Finland: THE THREE RIVER VALLEYS

The Ice Age designed intricate networks and waterways, inlets and rapids with its massive glaciers, leaving great hollows and narrow moraine ridges where mountains stood before. Reminders of the frozen era are the thousands of lakes and islands that provide one of the best recreational areas in all of Europe. The beauty of this region is in its unspoiled, magnificent forests and countryside with charming little towns that dot the waterways and lakesides. There's boating, swimming, fishing and hiking.

The industrial city of Tampere is the center of the Kokemäki River Valley. There is a Byzantine Eastern Orthodox Church, many art museums, a zoo, and dolphinarium among other things to see.

Lahti, known for its huge ski jumps that are used for international and national competitions every winter, is a center for other winter sports as well. At the end of Lake Päijänne Waterway, whose shores are fjord-like, is Jyväskylä, a university and teacher-college town, where there is a museum in honor of Alvar Aalto, the famous architect.

The third of the river valleys is the Saimaa Waterway whose center is at Lappeenranta with its many historical monuments that depict a colorful past. On this waterway are two other eastern Finland cities: Savonlinna, with its international Opera Festival, and Kuopio, known for its fish bakes and as the Marshall Mannerheim headquarters during the war. Kuopio also has the Museum of the Orthodox Church (unique in the Western World), an open air museum, and a week-long dance and music festival late in June.

Bothnia, on the coast of the Gulf of Bothnia, is an area of flatland through which several rivers run into the gulf. In the summer at harvest time, it is a sea of grain fields and drying barns. In the spring, it often suffers from flooding. It is also the area through which the trains run on their way to Lapland's ski resorts. In spots on the coast, there are still Finns whose home language is Swedish. Bothnia or Pohjanmaa is where many Finnish Americans have their roots. Notable in Bothnia are its folk music festivals, such as the Kaustinen Folk Festival that has become world famous. (See Festivals.)

The coastal towns of Uusikaupunki, Kristiinankaupunki, Vaasa, Uusikaarlepyy, Kokkola, Raahe, and Oulu share the sea, but each has its individual history: Other towns on the coast are a part of Lapland, such as Kemi and Tornio which lie on the "waist line" of the Maiden of Finland, the narrowest part of Finland. Her head is almost at the Arctic Ocean, and her right arm is in Norway. The Russians took her other arm which contained the nickel mines and the Murmansk Harbor which never freezes over because of the Gulf Stream from the Gulf of Mexico.

Rovaniemi, the capital of Lapland, is its center of travel. Destroyed in the war, its rebuilding was designed by Architect Alvar Aalto. The streets are laid out in the shape of a pair of reindeer antlers. Santa Claus lives there and his elves work in the castle Murr-Murr. Arktikum, a multi-disciplinary science center, is also an attraction. As the gateway of Lapland, tours are operated from Rovaniemi.

A few thousand Sami people still herd reindeer in Lapland. Some still live a nomadic way of life. For the summer the reindeer are driven up on the fells (mountains) to escape the vicious mosquitoes. All the reindeer need for food is lichen which they dig up even in great depths of snow. Many Sami families travel as far as Norway in the summer; international borders are no barrier. Herding reindeer has become commercialized, and few

Lapps live the way they used to in their teepees when the reindeer provided them with meat, milk, and furs for clothing and shelter.

There are many ski resorts in Lapland: some are company owned, others are private enterprises. In addition to snow and skiing, Lapland offers uncrowded living, vast horizons, two months of darkness around Christmas called *kaamos,* and fascinating northern lights — the mystical dance of the Aurora Borealis.

My husband Chico and I visited Lapland in January, 1998, a time when *kaamos* (the dark) was on its way out. The days were still short, and lights were turned on at two p.m. Earlier in the day, the sun, coming back from its long vacation, seemed to shine with extra brightness directly in our eyes as we tried to guide two reindeer along a path on a frozen lake in Kittilä.

We experienced the magic of Lapland as we watched skiers skiing downhill off the Lapland fells and as we chanted *(joikua)* to the beat of Sami drums around a roaring fire in a tepee. A magic was created by the Sami people in their colorful dress, with shirts and boots made of reindeer skin, and by the language of the musher speaking to his husky team as we gathered around the *kota* fire eating reindeer stew.

My special wish was to see the northern lights once more. Twilight had settled in; the stars came out and made the snowy village glow. It was a soft, gentle darkness during our last night at Levi Fell. Just as we came out of our sauna, we received a call that the show in the sky was on! Green veils of light danced above the fell with blue streaks of light joining in…this was the universe itself! That was the most magical moment of all — the Aurora Borealis. My wish and fantasy were fulfilled.

FESTIVALS IN FINLAND

General Music Festivals

Often the visits by American Finns to Finland are concentrated on meeting with relatives and friends in impeccable homes or summer villas by the lake, where they consume incredible amounts of coffee and *pulla* and salmon with tiny, delicious potatoes with dill on top. To add to these occasions, one might plan to take in some of the many musical events around which one's friends and relatives could gather. Summer music festivals are planned early in the year, and can be an enjoyable highlight for all involved.

As you will see, there is an incredible choice of music festivals in Finland every summer to suit every musical taste. Several kinds of music festivals are held in Finland: Chamber Music, General Music, Opera Festivals, Jazz Festivals, Rock Festivals, and "Other Music Festivals." Most of these take place in the summer, but there are a few exceptions:

The Oulu Chamber Music Festival is in March as is the **Hetta Chamber Music Festival** in Enontekiö, Lapland. There is the **April Jazz Espoo** near Helsinki, and one in Kainuu, Lapland in May. It seems skiing has been suggested to go along with these early Lapland festivals! Tampere offers **"Tampere Jazz Happening"** in November, and Lahti has an **Organ Festival** in August.

As a child I remember my parents and their friends attending the Sortavala Song Festival, which was a summer highlight for them. Now that Sortavala is Russian property, the songfest

I attended was held in Joensuu, in the Finnish Karelia, quite a few summers ago.

The Joensuu Festival Week

The Joensuu Festival in June provides many musical treats: opera, dance, world music and rock music alike. The theme for the 1997 festival was "The World Around the Corner," and it stressed the interaction in the musical world. It presented many international performers and music by international composers. For instance, American conductor Michael Christie conducted the Helsinki Philharmonic Orchestra, and Lynn Harrell was the cello soloist. The Finnish international soprano Karita Mattila performed her newest repertoire.

The Sysmä Summer Sounds

This festival, in the heart of scenic Häme province, presents a dozen or more concerts of both classical and Finnish traditional music. Most of the events take place in Sysmä's idyllic churches and manor houses, but the program of lighter music is performed in Finland's only Opera Barn, with the best-known Finnish stars.

The Mikkeli Music Festival

The program at the Mikkeli Music Festival consists of many concerts ranging from intimate recitals to full-scale opera productions. Maestro Valery Gergiev and the choir and soloists of the St. Petersburg Mariinsky Theatre are often the principal performers. Other foreign, as well as top Finnish performers, are featured. This festival takes place in the beautiful Finnish Lake District.

The Turku Music Festival

This festival is held in August in Turku, the oldest Finnish town, whose historic buildings and architecture provide an excellent environment for musical performances. The varied program includes orchestral concerts, string quartets, chamber music, medieval, renaissance and baroque music, as well as chamber opera.

The Helsinki Festival

The Helsinki Festival comprises a series of first-rate classical musical events interwoven with a varied multi-arts program. The music ranges from classical music — both new and old — to jazz, world music and rock. The great names in today's dance are found there, as are paintings, and visual artists working with new technology. This festival is a meeting of cultures; artistic experiences abound. The award-winning Huvila (Villa) Tent is the heartbeat of the Festival, featuring many events in a growing variety of styles. And of course, look for Kantele Concerts — the 2000-year-old, traditional Finnish stringed instrument — in the Finnish capital while there. In 1997, Timo Väänänen was chosen the "Young Artist of the Year."

OPERA FESTIVALS

The Savonlinna Opera Festival

Perhaps the best-known summer extravaganza in Finland is the Savonlinna Opera Festival in July-August. It takes place in the province of Savo, in the medieval castle of Olavinlinna. Surrounded by water, it was built in 1475 as a stronghold and has been an administrative center of eastern Finland for centuries.

There are art and industrial art exhibits during the opera

week. Both Savonlinna and Olavinlinna are located on a separate island in the beautiful Saimaa waterway, and a romantic cruise can be taken along the Saimaa lake system.

Ilmajoki Music Festival
Another opera festival in Finland is the Ilmajoki Festival in Vaasa, located on the western coast of Finland. A Finnish production is traditionally performed there, in addition to a large number of concerts and other events during the festival period.

CHAMBER MUSIC FESTIVALS

Of the eleven annual Chamber Music Festivals held in Finland, there are three special coastal town concerts:

Naantali Music Festival
This festival is an international chamber music festival in Finland's most popular vacation spot. The main concert is held in Naantali's 15th-century abbey; other concerts are held in old churches in nearby districts. Both Finnish and a variety of visiting foreign artists are among the performers. An outdoor concert is held in the garden of the Finnish president's summer residence in Naantali.

The Avanti! Summer Sounds
The Avanti! Chamber Orchestra's Summer Sounds, in the historic town of Porvoo, presents a broad spectrum of both classical and modern music, that ranges from ensembles to a full symphony orchestra. There are many foreign soloists and guest artists. Among them have been conductor Esa-Pekka Salonen from the Los Angeles Philharmonic Orchestra, and composer Henri Dutilleux from France.

The Kangasniemi Music Festival

This festival provides concerts and first-rate training for singers, pianists and players of stringed instruments. The Kangasniemi Singing Competition provides an opportunity for young singers to test their abilities, while the Poleen Lied piano competition at Pieksämäki tests the pianists' talents. Performers at the concerts include winners of international singing competitions. Kangasniemi is located southeast of Pieksämäki.

The Crusell Week in Uusikaupunki

The Crusell Week in July emphasizes woodwind music. Held in the beautiful west coast town of Uusikaupunki, it provides a recital competition for woodwind players, as well as chamber music and orchestral concerts. One event is a "Cruise Concert" and another the "Night of the Lanterns." Master classes are organized for flute, oboe, clarinet and bassoon.

Other Chamber Music Festivals

Oulu Music Festival features music, from Bach to contemporary Chinese, in soloist recitals, chamber ensemble concerts, and full symphonic concerts by many well-known Finnish orchestras.

Riihimäki Summer Concerts are performed during the week preceding the Midsummer celebration, in the unique atmosphere of the Finnish Museum of Glass Exhibition Hall, which has magnificent acoustics. A group of accomplished artists perform, and there are many free concerts, in addition to night concerts, and special events for children. The Glass Museum contains 17,000 objects, among them a 2000-year old Syrian tear-bottle.

Time of Music at Viitasaari, located in central Finland, is where a score of well-known composers such as Mauricio Kagel, Jean-Claude Risset, Alvin Lucier, Iannis Xenakis, George Crumb, and others have left their mark. Well-known ensembles and musicians from all over the world perform.

Oulainen Music Week, held in early November in the northern Ostrobothnian town of Oulainen, offers top quality concerts to suit a variety of tastes from light music to sacred, and from folk music to classical.

Hetta Music Event takes place in March during the most important gathering of the Sami people among the snowy hills of Lapland's Kalott region. The Hetta event features sacred and early Baroque music. Excellent opportunity exists for combining music, winter sports, and learning about the lifestyle of the Lapps. In the church village of Hetta, the Easter sun can be enjoyed both physically and spiritually. Winners of different musical contests perform, including artists of the Saami cultural heritage.

JAZZ FESTIVALS

The Pori Jazz

The first Pori Jazz festival was organized in 1966 by local jazz enthusiasts: students, journalists and musicians. Tens of thousands of tourists come to Pori to enjoy jazz or just to have a good time. This festival has become the second largest in Europe, and has presented such artists as Benny Goodman, Sarah Vaughan, Miles Davis, Fats Domino and Dizzy Gillespie to Finland. However, in the 80s, the program began to include rock, rhythm and blues purely for economic reasons, but 90 percent of the music played at Pori is still jazz. Now that the European Union recognizes Pori Jazz as an international event, they have been generous with their support. A new concert arena is being built at Raatimiehenluoto because of the growth of Pori Jazz. Finnish jazz has reached a professional level since the Sibelius Academy and Oulunkylä's Conservatory started teaching it.

Kainuu Jazz Spring

This is a four-day, international event in May. The music program varies from acoustic jazz to the electric atmosphere of the clubs. Some world class artists have visited Kajaani: Arturo Sandoval, Dizzy Gillespie, Charlie Haden and Phil Woods. Programs are performed in the Kaukametsä Concert Hall and on the three stages of the Kajanus Hotel. The free admission events in the town center are the backbone of the festival. The atmosphere of Kainuu Jazz Spring is exhilarating during the springtime awakening of the tundra.

Lakeside Blues Festival in Järvenpää

Held just north of Helsinki, this long-established festival has free concerts, children's events, and club evenings downtown. The main event is a picnic style happening for the whole family on the shores of Lake Tuusula.

Kalott Jazz and Blues Festival

In Tornio and Haaparanta, twin border towns, this is the largest jazz festival of the far north. Both Finnish and Swedish cultures come together in the sunlit days and nights of the north. International rhythms and melodies are heard in concert halls, in jazz tents, in the streets and in town squares. Top-notch jazz artists from all over the world perform.

Baltic Jazz, Marine Jazz Festival

Taalintehdas, in southwestern Finland, provides an impression of Sea Finland. The best of the Baltic jazz musicians are present at this festival. There many events; some of them, free of charge, are presented in a charming, historic factory setting on seven different stages. In addition, there are traditional outdoor and evening concerts and jam sessions. Special features include chamber jazz, children's jazz, jazz cruises and a church service with jazz music.

ROCK FESTIVALS

Provinssi Rock

Seinäjoki hosts one of the two rock festivals held in Finland. The festival is a three-day event with top class programming by Finnish and foreign performers. There is also an opportunity to enjoy theatrical and other performances within the festival area, which is located on the beautiful island of Törnävänsaari. Good quality food services are available.

Nummi Rock

At Kauhajoki, Nummijärvi, there is a three-day festival of the finest Finnish and international rock music. The festival is held in a scenic park, on the sandy shores of Lake Nummijärvi. There is parking and camping and, of course, top quality programming.

OTHER MUSIC FESTIVALS

The Kaustinen Folk Music Festival

This is perhaps the best known of the folk music festivals in Finland, with the exception, perhaps, of the Savonlinna Opera Festival. The celebration of folk music and Nordic dance transforms Kaustinen into a global village with performers and visitors from such faraway places as Taiwan, Puerto Rico, Scotland and Tanzania. The village of 3,600 fills with as many as 82,000 visitors in and around its center, Aapintalo. The Finnish government assisted in establishing the center, after recognizing the incredible increase of interest in folk music.

The Kaustinen Festival celebrated its 30th Anniversary in 1997 with a concert series encompassing the most outstanding performances of folk music and dance. The folk musical "Henrik" was presented in the new folk art center concert hall. Over 3000 Finnish musicians performed, including master folk musicians, world music bands, dance companies, and singer-songwriters.

There are exhibitions and happenings of all varieties taking place in restaurants, outdoor amphitheaters, and on monument steps. The faithful flock there each summer, and among them, Oren Tikkanen, the musician and teacher, who writes a music column for *The Finnish American Reporter*. The next millenium has already begun at Kaustinen!

Tango Festival at Seinäjoki

This is a boisterous, well-organized summer event for tens of thousands of festival-goers in the heart of town. "The magic of the tango goes straight to the heart and touches the soul," they say. At Seinäjoki, on the world's largest asphalt dance floor, there's room for 20,000 dancers! You can listen to the finest concerts and attend the finals of the singing contest to select the King and the Queen of the Tango at the Sports Hall. There is more dancing at the Atria Hall just a few minutes away.

In addition to the these listings there is an **International Choir Festival** at Tampere, an **Accordion Festival** at Ikaalinen, the **Kihaus Folk Music Festival** at Rääkkylä, a **Brass Week** at Lieksa, a **Festival of Workers' Music** at Valkeakoski, and an **Organ Festival** in Lahti.

DANCE, THEATRE AND LITERATURE FESTIVALS

Finns have always been stage-struck and avid theater-goers. A large number of amateur and professional theaters are active in Finland, a characteristic which Finnish Americans have kept dear to their hearts.

Finland's Kivi Festival

This festival takes place at Nurmijärvi, just thirty miles north of Helsinki. It is the birthplace of Aleksis Kivi, the beloved author of the play "Seven Brothers." This play, about the struggle of seven rowdy backwoods brothers, is performed at Nurmijärvi in the longest running summer festival in Finland. Hundreds of amateur actors have participated in this dramatic interplay of taming the brothers as well as the wilderness. The different characters struggle among themselves to keep things as they are, yet, at the same time, each wants to find a girl to marry. In order to marry, the brothers need to learn to read and then to have their first communion. (The Lutheran Church of Finland required this.) Meanwhile in the woods, while renting out their home, they begin to work furiously and clear a good amount of land, and are better off for it.

A VARIETY OF FESTIVALS

There are at least ten happenings in Dance, Theater, and Literature throughout Finland! Choices include: an Amateur Theater Festival, a Schottische Festival, a Children's Festival, a Dance Festival, a Comic Festival, and a Poetry and Music Festival. Some are listed here:

The Häme Castle Children's Festival
For twenty years the medieval castle of Häme has opened its doors to life, offering new and fascinating worlds of experience to its audiences. Hämeenlinna is just a two-hour drive north of Helsinki. It is Jean Sibelius's hometown and has a museum dedicated to the famous composer. The festival celebrates families and children with a program of drama, puppet theater, dance, concerts, exhibitions, workshops and films. Close by is the Aulanko Park and resort with wonderful lakes and sports facilities.

The Bomba Festival in Nurmes
Located in the Finnish Karelia, this festival is unique because it delves into the Finno-Ugrian culture in an International Theater Festival. The program includes performances in music, dance, thematic evenings in the festival tent, street theater, exhibitions, and seminars. In addition to Finnish performers there are those from Hungary, Estonia, Russia, Sweden and Norway.

Words and Music in Kajaani
This is a poetry week in the town of Kajaani by Lake Oulujärvi. In 1997, Finnish character was on display in numerous presentations honoring Finland's 80th anniversary of inde-

pendence. This event gathers well-known Finnish poets and those who recite poetry, as well as newcomers. Finnish popular music, films, and dance are an integral part of the program.

The Pispala Schottische Dance Mania
In this festival at Tampere's Pispala, new folk dances and music are celebrated. In the whirl of Dance Mania, international performers from East and West encounter the Finnish tradition along with those who are trying it out for the first time and those who are experienced enthusiasts. The energetic jam sessions and dance evenings give everyone a chance to get first hand experience. The festival is organized by the Association of Youth Clubs and the city of Tampere.

The Pentinkulma Days
Pentinkulma Days at Urjala, just west of Hämeenlinna, the birthplace of Väinö Linna, author of the beloved epic novel *Here Under the North Star.* This festival attracts many writers, literary professionals and enthusiasts. It also provides a variety of programs for friends of culture with its courses and seminars and first-rate public events. There is entertainment on dance floors, and in restaurants; there are theater productions and exhibitions.

MORE FESTIVALS IN THIS GROUP

The Amateur Dramatics Festival at Seinäjoki, in July.

The International Amateur Theater at Mikkeli, in January.

The Arctic Comics Festival in Kemi, in March.

FOLK FESTIVALS

Jutalaiset in Rovaniemi, the largest festival of folk dance and music in the Northern Kalott region, brings together the young, as well as the older Juta to enjoy music and dance in the nightless night of Lapland. Well-known performers from Lapland and elsewhere in Finland, as well as representatives from other European minority groups, perform at this festival. The Jutalaiset, with its many side shows under the midnight sun, creates an unique ambience that spreads across the entire Rovaniemi district — its streets, squares, hills and lakesides, restaurants, tents and stages. It is celebration of nature as well!

Eteläpohjalaiset Spelit at Karijoki and Kristiinankaupunki

An old seafaring town, with its wooden house precincts and alleys and its Wolf Cave archaeological find at Pyhävuori, creates an exciting backdrop for this international and provincial grand happening of folk music, dance and song.

Joutsa Folk Festival

In the middle of Finland's lake district by the idyllic Lake Suontee, east of Mikkeli, the Joutsa Festival presents heritage shows, exhibitions, a children's festival, and a church boat show. Summer festival competitions are also part of this program. Finnish performers are joined by visiting groups. Events include modern heritage, for example, a rock concert for the young. Concerts performed on the stages at the church and open-air museum emphasize classical and children's music.

The Kymenlaakso Folk Art and Folk Music Festival

This festival happens in Miehikkälä, a small town not far from Viipuri on the Russian side. While the program is different each summer, the atmosphere is that of a Karelian folk music and dance festival, which invites you to come and enjoy the sounds in the town's surroundings and light summer nights.

ART CENTERS AND OTHER PLACES TO SEE

Along with festivals, many of the following places are of special interest:

The Retretti Art Center at Punkaharju

Not far from Savonlinna, where you might have enjoyed an opera in the medieval castle of Olavinlinna, you can stop to visit the Retretti Art Center that is located in an underground grotto. It has regular exhibitions of major works of art. In 1997 there was a magnificent display of Matisse's early work. In 1996 Russian art was displayed, most on loan from Russian collections. Concerts are also performed at the Retretti, and tours are available when booked in advance. Retretti is one of the most beautiful settings in Finland, on the Punkaharju Ridge — the view of the ribbons of lakes and islands is unlimited!

The Salmela Arts Center

This art center is located at Mäntyharju, south of Mikkeli, on lovely Lake Saimaa. There is a multi-art cultural exhibition in the beautiful church village milieu of Salmela. Top glass art exhibitions take place at Iso-Pappila. Concerts are also performed in the wooden church which seats 2,000 people. Lectures by well-known philosophers, and recitals of music by talented opera singers and performers are held here, as well.

PERFORMING GROUPS

Värttinä

Värttinä is a group of Finland's folk musicians who are best known abroad, thanks to their many tours in Europe and the U.S.A. Having studied at the Sibelius Academy, this group has won a wide international reputation. They have produced many recordings, such as "Oi Dai," which is a step further from the traditional and "Seleniko," which is Värttinä's top-ten Billboard World Album. Four women sing the vocals in beautiful harmony. Eight instrumentalists play an array of instruments: fiddle, accordion, kantele, trumpet, bass, percussion, tenor banjo, saxophone, bouzouki, kaval, tin whistle, domra! One song, "Lemmennosto," is an old magic rune in which Värttinä casts a musical love spell in 7/8 and 6/8 time.
Translated:
> "Fire up, young man's heart!
> I will put a flame on your hips.
> If you don't care I will swear
> and conjure up the flames of
> love. May the lovers have good
> fortune and many children!"

Tallari

The Tallari group was established in 1986 in connection with the Kaustinen Foundation and the Kaustinen Folk Music Institute. There are six members playing fiddles, pump organ, accordions and wind instruments. Each player also "doubles, triples, quadruples" by playing instruments such as the jouhikko, guitar, mandolin, bass, and kantele. There is a vocal component also.

Risto Hotakainen and Ritva Talvitie are are two of the original players — Risto plays the fiddle and bass, jouhikko, mandolin and "nyckelharpa." Ritva kept one foot in the folk music realm while simultaneously studying classical music. In Tallari she plays the jouhikko and the two-row button accordion. A student of the Sibelius Academy, she played in the orchestra of the Finnish National Opera, and teaches at the Ostrobothnian Conservatory.

Some Tallari recordings are: "Komiammasti," spotlighting greatest hits of the past along with new ones. "Ten-Cent Drink" *(Kymmenen pennin ryyppy)* has traditional tunes and is a creative presentation of the richness of pure Finnish folk music. "The Maiden Who Was Redeemed" *(Lunastettava Neito)* features Saami, Votyak and Karelian music and songs from the *Kanteletar.*

Veli-Matti Järvenpää

With his multi-sized accordions, Veli-Matti's Tex-Mex Quartet, with Tero Pulkkinen, Ville Tolonen, and Jukka-Pekka Nieminen, is one of the top entertainments at not only the Kaustinen Folk Festival but at many other summer festivals in Finland also.

One of the Veli-Matti Quartet's compact disc releases is *Pitkä Hehku* (Lasting Glow). Some of the songs are: "Forget the Tears," "It's the Woman's Fault," and "The Forgotten Ones."

SOME FINNISH-AMERICAN MUSICIANS

Singing Strings

Singing Strings is a group of young musicians, ages seven to nineteen, who study under Helinä Pakola at her Evergreen School of Performing Arts in Virginia, Minnesota. Ms. Pakola studied at the Sibelius Academy in Helsinki, but teaches violin using the Suzuki method. Singing Strings has performed at many "FinnFests," delighting audiences time after time with light classical and Finnish folk music. The group also sings in Finnish, and is exposed to other Finnish cultural aspects at school. They present an exciting and authentic program in their colorful costumes, accompanied by Hilpi Leino-Kantola and Helinä Pakola.

The Singing Strings' reputation earned an official invitation to perform in Finland at the Kaustinen Folk Festival, the Ivalo Festival, International Doctors' Concert at the Savonlinna Opera Festival, at the Gala Event of the Finland Society in Helsinki, and at a Benefit Concert with the First Lady Mrs. Eeva Ahtisaari.

Merja Soria

Merja Soria studied classical accordion at the Conservatory of Helsinki, Ethnomusicology at the University of Helsinki, and folk music at the Sibelius Academy. Merja, a teacher of Finnish music at two San Diego colleges, moved there in 1988. Her "non-Finnish" ensemble playing Finnish folk music, is well-known at "FinnFests," where her kantele and accordion concerts, and her singing are much enjoyed. Merja was the first "Performer of the Year" chosen by the Finlandia Foundation in 1996, and subsequently she toured the country giving many concerts. Merja's music video, "Spirits of the Past," was filmed in Finland's idyllic summer surroundings.

Koivun Kaiku

Koivun Kaiku ("Echo of the Birch") is a kantele ensemble in Minnesota. A dozen performers play from 5-string to 41-string kanteles, flutes, accordion, birchbark Repo flute, and spoons. Directed by Joyce Hakala, the ensemble plays "Songs

From Metsola," a collection of Finnish folk songs by Marjorie Edgar, who was captivated by the beautiful, sometimes plaintive melodies of the immigrants. Through their songs and traditions, she learned to understand the Finnish people's spiritual ties to the north woods and to the ancient mythology of their homeland.

Koivun Kaiku was chosen as the Performer(s) of the Year in 1997 by the Finlandia Foundation. They have performed at several "FinnFests" and travel around the country performing in Finnish American communities. I have their delightful cassette of "Songs from Metsola."

Melvin Kangas

Melvin Kangas is a talented, well-known musician, actor, and playwright, who has been noted as playing the kantele better than anyone else in the U.S.A. As a playwright, he wrote an electronic music drama about Lemminkäinen, a *Kalevala* hero, for the Hancock "FinnFest II." As an actor he played in "Susipari," ("Wolf Pair") a play based on Kalle Päätalo's drama by the same name.

Gerry Luoma Henkel

Gerry Luoma Henkel is a kantele maker who loves every kantele he makes. He has toured the country promoting other Finnish and Finnish-American musicians, and was the tour manager in 1986 for the internationally known folk/jazz band "Karelia." Gerry gives workshops and lectures wherever he goes.

DANCE MUSIC BY FINNISH AMERICANS

Old-time Favorites
Viola Turpeinen is a legend. Her accordion music of polkas, schottisches, waltzes, folksongs, and tangos is still heard and loved in Finnish-American communities. Her "Songs and Dances" is available in five volumes and on recordings with other artists.
Arthur Kylander played in the Finn Halls for decades. Recordings of his humorous songs and dance tunes such as *"Oi Kuinka Engeliksi Mielin"* are available labeled "Finnish-American Recordings II."
Ernest Paananen is one of the greats of old-time music. *"Naimahommia,"* "Finnish-American Recordings III," has his popular repertoire of Finnish folk music.

Ameriikan Poijat
This group has its roots in the Finnish Army band, and is a well-known group that appears at Finnish-American gatherings, such as "FinnFest" dances. Their music has a distinctly Finnish sound, as heard on "Finnish Brass in America," which is old dance music typically played by a seven-piece band in the late 19th and early 20th centuries.

Oulu Hotshots
The Oulu Hotshots is a three-member band from Ironriver, Wisconsin, that plays polkas, mazurkas, waltzes, *humppas* and *raatikko* with continuous energy. They also play slow pieces, which attract a consistently large crowd at "FinnFest" dances. They have played in Finland, too. Several recordings of their music are available, one for instance, "Oulu Hotshots #1" has "Northern Images," "Bringin' It Back," and "Northern Lights."

Oren Tikkanen

Oren Tikkanen is a wise, informative musician and writer. As a columnist for *Finnish American Reporter*, he gives insight into the people, their music and instruments. He travels far and wide to hear individuals and groups perform in the U.S.A. and in Finland, often "jamming" with them. He plays a variety of instruments with the "Thimbleberry Hi-Lighters" and other groups, and shares his love of music.

"Reunion at Finntown" is a recording by Tikkanen and Friends that features old-time Finn Hall music. Many of these songs were written in the 20s and 30s.

"Children of the Finnish Immigrant," a recording of music by five second generation Finnish-American singers and musicians of Michigan's Upper Peninsula, has John Perona and Oren Tikkanen as accompanists.

"Al Reko and Oren Tikkanen Dance at the Finn Hall" features sixteen traditional Finnish dance tunes played in Finn Halls across America. Included are *Villiruusu* ("Wild Rose") and *Metsäkukkia* ("Forest Flowers"), two loved old melodies. (*Metsäkukkia* has been recorded by a number of well-known folk musicians, including Jay Ungar and Molly Mason.)

Oren Tikkanen dedicated "Life in the Finnish-American Woods," with Al Reko, to composers William Syrjälä, Arthur Kylander, Hiski Salomaa and Antti Syrjäniemi. The dedication says, "whose songs sustained immigrant families; and to Viola Turpeinen, whose playing inspired us all."

Bobby Vee

Bobby Vee's last name is Velline (Wellin), and he is from Fargo, North Dakota — almost a hometown boy for the Minot "FinnFest," where he was well received! He tells the story that his success as a professional musician was promoted because of a tragic airplane crash in which four members of his band perished. The subsequent notoriety gave Bobby's career, at fifteen, a boost. Three of his sons also perform in his band "The Vees." At the "FinnFest," they played mostly old and tame rock-and-roll, delighting the audience.

Conga Se Mene
This group plays "Finnish Reggae and Sauna Beats" plus other exotic beats and rhythms. "Land of the Conga Boys" includes Finnish reggae and Northern Isle rock and sauna beats!

OTHER FINNISH AMERICAN PERFORMING GROUPS

Finnish-American Singers of Michigan
The Finnish-American Singers of Michigan is a group that has performed at thirteen "FinnFests." As well as Finns, the group consists of people of many backgrounds, including: German, Italian, Japanese, and Polish.

Kisarit Dancers
This group was formed in 1972 and specializes in Finnish folk dance. Usually there are eight couples and the musicians, mostly from the Minneapolis area. Their leader is Kathy Jackson. They are known and appreciated by "FinnFest" goers.

***Kalevala* Theater Society**
The *Kalevala* Society's home is in Virginia, on the Iron Range in northern Minnesota. At the Minot "FinnFest," they premiered Margaret Webster's play "The Aurora and the Red Moon," which recounts life in the North during ancient times in terms of legends, relationships and actions. The play, directed by H. Michael Loy, was written from the point of view of Louhi, Mistress of the North, from the *Kalevala*.

Medieval Churches in the Finnish Southwest

There is a fantastic one-day bus tour of medieval churches in the southwestern part of Finland in the Turku region. This summertime tour can be arranged at almost any time as long as there are twenty people in the group.

Christianity was brought to Finland from Sweden via the town of Turku in the 11th century by Bishop Henry. In time, Finland was converted to Catholicism, which, in many ways, benefitted the country. Many churches were constructed, as were castles for defending the country against intruders that came from all directions, mostly in search of furs.

The Finnish churches, having been in use ever since their establishment, have seen history in the making and therefore have suffered wear and tear that has necessitated countless repairs and renovations. The walls of the churches that originally had frescoes, for instance, were painted over by the Protestant Reformation, which believed people should be reading the Bible on their own instead of learning Bible stories from the painted interpretations on the church walls. Some churches in remote villages, and especially on the islands, however, did escape the dictum to remove the paintings. The Hattula, Espoo, and Ahvenanmaa churches are examples that still have the frescoes.

The stone churches now have vaulted ceilings which were added in the 15th and 16th centuries. It is easy to see, however, that much of the original fabric and artifacts remain.

Due to the closeness to the sea, common elements in coastal stone churches (also in Sweden and Norway) are beautiful model ships hanging from the ceiling, most dating back to the 18th and 19th centuries. The regions depended on the sea and must have depended on the blessings of the church, too.

Other common elements are standards bearing coats-of-arms of the noble families — these decorate the walls of each parish. Before the 18th century, there was usually an hourglass on the pulpit, to remind the preacher to limit his preachings. These hourglasses were eventually replaced by tall case clocks.

The Askainen parish church is a lovely stone church built by the great Fleming family, who also built the nearby Louhisaari Manor. The present church was built between 1650 and 1653 by Admiral Herman Klaus von Fleming to replace a decaying old wooden chapel. Askainen was originally part of Lemu parish. The first mention of a chapel in the parish dates from 1592, but one of its bells in the present church is dated 1548, so the chapel must have been older. A stained glass window in the church is believed to have been salvaged from the old chapel.

The new church is in neoclassical style with pointed arches, reflecting the tastes of the nobility. The ceiling consists of three octagonal star vaults, supported by two spans. The porch and the beautifully carved wooden pulpit were brought from Germany as war booty by Herman Fleming, who was admiral of the Swedish fleet during the Thirty-Years War. On the walls are several family coats-of-arms from the 17th century. Twenty-two members of the Fleming family are interred in a burial chamber beneath the church.

Early in the 19th century, Louhisaari Manor passed into the ownership of the Mannerheim family, whose mausoleum in the churchyard houses the graves of Marshall Mannerheim and several earlier generations of the Mannerheims. One of the chandeliers in the church was donated by Marshall

Mannerheim. The detached bell tower was built in 1790 by a famous church builder, Mikael Piimänen.

The Merimasku church, a wooden church is the newest of the churches. It was probably built in the late 17th century, and is still in use. The churchyard is beautiful, as are all churchyards and cemeteries in Finland (and Scandinavia). They are awe-inspiring gardens, many dating back to the 17th century. To see a churchyard or cemetery bedecked with flowers and entirely aglow with candles on Independence Day and on Christmas Eve is an unforgettable experience.

The large and high Convent Church of Naantali is a mid-16th century convent church of the Order of St. Bridget *(Pyhä Birgitta)* that was founded in Finland in 1438. The convent *Villa Gratiae* began its work in the village of Masku, but soon afterwards took over the farmhouse of Ailoinen in the parish of Raisio. In 1443, King Kristoffer of Denmark, Sweden and Norway authorized moving the convent to Naantali, but the church, the only surviving monastic building, was not consecrated until 1462.

At the entrance of the church there are two wood sculptures, one of Mary holding the dead body of Jesus, and the other probably of St. Catherine of Alexandria. In a glass case, there is an altar cloth made by the nuns, most likely dating from the 16th century. A four-branched iron candlestick on top of the case is also dated from monastic times. Hanging from the ceiling in front of the case is the Consecration Crown, beneath which the novice took her final vows. Nearby stands a tall, Gothic-style monstrance, with iron framework, dating back to 1369, that was used for exposition of the Sacred Host in Catholic times.

The *Pieta* painting, possibly a work of El Greco, was donated by Queen Katarina Jagellonica to the convent. Near the altar is a carved wooden crucifix made by the monks of Naantali.

The only original wall paintings to survive the Reformation are the four consecration crosses on each end wall. The beautiful brightly colored Renaissance pulpit was a gift from Henry Fleming in 1622; both its date and origin are unknown. The triptych above the present altar is of Swedish origin and is late 15th century work. The central wood carving represents the crowning of Mary as Queen of Heaven. On her right is St. Bridget in her habit, and on her left, St. Bridget's daughter Katarina. The small carvings on either side represent the twelve apostles and four saints. Beneath the triptych is the most precious work of art in the church: an exquisite small wood carving, by an unknown master, of the head of Christ crowned with thorns.

The St. Martin's Church in Raisio is a single-nave graystone and wooden church built in 1305. It has been renovated several times. In 1650, the wooden vaulted roof was built, and wall frescoes painted over. The present Baroque-style pulpit was brought from Riga, probably as war booty. In the past the church contained some extraordinary medieval art, such as paintings of St. Martin and the Apostle Simon, as well as carved wooden sculptures of Mary, St. Anne and others; all are currently displayed in the National Museum in Helsinki. The most valuable work of art is the great triumph crucifix by the Master of Lieto, an unknown 14th-century woodcarver from a nearby village. The last renovation occurred in 1989, when a modern balcony with staircase was erected to support the 20-register organ. On display in a glass case are two valuable books: *Missale Aboense,* the 1492 missal of the Turku Diocese, and the first Finnish edition of the *Holy Bible* that dates from 1641.

The Church of St. Henry at Nousiainen is, after the Cathedral of Turku, undoubtedly the most important medieval church in Finland. Historical research and national tradition agree and place the martyrdom of St. Henry in the year 1166, and it is known that he was buried at Nousiainen.

The first reliable mention of the church was in the 1232, but this, as well as subsequent records, refers not to the present church, but to a smaller church, probably built of wood. After coming to Finland in 1286, Bishop Johannes I simultaneously initiated the construction of both the cathedral and the church at Nousiainen. Brick and stone are the predominant building materials in both churches. Several changes in the building plans were made and the construction of the two-aisle church was completed by Bishop Maunu II Tavast in the early 15th century. Its most priceless possession is the sarcophagus of St. Henry, given by the bishop himself. A few of the frescoes escaped the Protestant reformers and are characterized by a certain primitiveness and robustness of design. As subjects of the pictures, different allegorical animal and human figures, geometrical arrangements, tree-of-life patterns, and also some coats-of-arms were chosen. On one of the pillars is a very ancient painting of a ship of the Viking type. The pulpit is decorated with paintings of Christ and five of the apostles. On the cover of the pulpit are the coats-of-arms of the donors in 1640.

There are two other old gray stone churches in this region. The Masku church is a typical gray-stone church from the 14th century, and the Lemu church is from the 16th century.

A friend that took a guided tour of this region suggests that one day is not sufficient time to take in completely the wealth of history and architecture in this region. One should allow a day and a half or two days.

The Evangelical Lutheran Church of Finland As I Saw It in 1997

There were tens of candles flickering as a group at the entrance, and many unlit ones for anyone wishing to offer a prayer, when I attended a church service in January 1997 at the Tapiola church. It was wonderful to feel the warmth and friendliness in the church!

Was this a sign of a return to old customs? The lighting of candles was a custom of the Catholic church when Finland, along with the Swedish Empire, was Catholic for over 200 years. It became Lutheran in the 1520s, with the Reformation, and still has approximately 4.3 million members. When the Pope's power switched to the King of Sweden, all the income and properties went to the king and his lords. Taxation became a burden. Even during the 100 years under the Russian Czars and their orthodox religion, Lutheranism remained the state church and was run by its supreme body, the Synod. Sermons were given in Finnish, and Mikael Agricola translated the New Testament into Finnish.

The Winter War of 1939-40 is said to have been characterized as a struggle for home, faith and fatherland. The church was a source of support and unity that was badly needed. The will to defend one's country had religious overtones. The financial independence of the church increased during the war, and after the war the church took on new tasks, for example, family counseling and youth work.

During the changes of the 60s, when people left their farms and moved to the cities, the church was branded too undemocratic and conservative. From the 70s on, however, discussion of ethics and ways of life has inspired increased interest in religion.

According to 1993 statistics, the Evangelical Lutheran Church of Finland has eight dioceses and about 600 independent parishes; the average parish has 7,000 members.

The Finnish Lutheran church now works with the youth and families. It maintains youth summer camps that have become learning centers for catechism in natural settings. It offers other social events such as coffee time after the service.

Church attendance is on the rise. The Tapiola church was crowded on the Sunday morning my sister and I attended, and to my surprise, people took communion without hesitation. In earlier days, one might hesitate. Not anymore! Women ministers help with the communion and at times do the service itself.

The church announces banns, the newborns, the dead, and church happenings. It performs first communions, baptisms and most of the weddings. It buries its dead and it still keeps records on all of its people.

The first of November is the traditional observation of All Saints' Day. The names of those who died after the first of November in the previous year are read in church; a candle is lit for each one and prayers are said. A choral program is offered, and by the main door of the church, there is a table for candles brought by individuals to light in memory of their loved ones. Tributes of flowers are also displayed. In a letter to the relatives of the deceased, Antti Rusama, the vicar for the Tapiola Parish at the time of our visit, suggested that those who were unable to come to church could observe a moment of remembrance at home with the lighting of a candle. The Vicar wrote, "Those who are sleeping their eternal sleep are close to us because love never disappears."

The hymnal was new to me, but with the support of the

great organ and a strong voice behind us, we joined in the singing. Coffee was served at the social hall after the service, which created a comfortable feeling of being welcome. The parishioners, including a good number of young people, greeted each other and visited.

My mother's generation, and the ones before her, marked time by the University of Helsinki's *Almanac,* which lists sixty three church-related days in red. For each of these days, the New Testament readings are listed. The farmers followed the *Almanac* religiously because they believed that the harvest depended on faith and the weather, and the weather on the movements of the heavenly bodies. Once in a while Mother — as she was reading the *Almanac* — would disappoint us by declaring, for instance, "The days are getting shorter," or on a certain day in August reporting, "Jaakko will throw a cold rock in the water tomorrow." The first remark meant "hurry up and make the most of the summer," the second signaled the end of the swimming season.

Even though Mother is no longer with us, I still check the *Almanac* for happenings in red and for the holidays with the corresponding quotes from the *Bible.* I find the listings at the end a valuable reference for possible names for grandchildren.

FINLAND NOW AND IN THE TWENTY-FIRST CENTURY

Finland today is more than a country of thousands of lakes and forests. Its tenacity or "sisu" shows in the fierce competition in technological advancements. The Nokia company, for instance, is a world leader in mobile and cellular phones, consumer electronics and telecommunication technology. One in five Finns has a cellular phone. One of Finnish technologies remarkable achievements is the self-organizing map, which is gaining recognition all over the world. Finnish instruments are on research probes in orbiter spacecraft. The SOHO, the European solar and heliospheric observatory satellite (1995), has the ERNE, a solar particle sensor developed in Finland, and a device called SWAN for observation of solar winds.

About two-thirds of Finland's surface area is covered with forests. The wood and paper industries and their quality products have made Finland known over the world. Finland still lives off its forests! Its paper-producing machinery that represents 21st century state-of-the-art equipment is an important export item. In addition to Nokia's electronics and the paper industry's products there are other Finnish products in the U.S. market, such as Marimekko fashions, Iittala and Nuutajärvi glass, Fiskars' scissors (now copied by the Japanese), Lappi-Cheese, Ry-Krisp hardtack, Rapala-fishing lures, ice-breakers, snowplows, and sauna heaters. Finland's Outokumpu Mining Company also exports smelter emission-cleansing technology. The quality of Finnish production has led to other countries seeking to "import" design and industrial engineers. The economy remains healthy with this spirit of industry.

NBC Nightly News reported, during President Clinton's and Russian President Yeltsin's Summit Meeting in Helsinki, that one third of the Finnish Parliament consisted of women — a woman, Riitta Uosukainen, is a very popular speaker of the parliament. Finland was the first European country to give universal and equal suffrage to women in 1906.

The Finns are avid readers and theater-goers, and they love sports. Old-time heroes, such as Paavo Nurmi and Lasse Viren, the long distance runners who won many gold medals in the Olympics of their time, are still revered. Ski jumping is near to Finnish hearts; many victories were won by young men, such as Toni Nieminen and Matti Nykänen, and there is new talent in the making. Fifteen Finnish hockey players are found in the National Hockey League, the best known are Jari Kurri and Teemu Selänne, both on the team at Anaheim, California.

Finland, now a member of the European Union, is a land of music and scores of summer music festivals that represent different regional cultures and are international competitive events. Outstanding performers include: opera stars Matti Salminen, Jorma Hynninen, and Karita Mattila; the internationally known music directors (conductors) Esa-Pekka Salonen of the Los Angeles Philharmonic and Jukka-Pekka Saraste in Toronto, and Pekka Kuusisto who, at nineteen, won the Sibelius Violin Contest in 1995. These are spectacular representatives of performers who follow in the footsteps of Jean Sibelius himself.

Although it is said that Finland is, perhaps, one of the most Americanized countries in Europe, it is still uncluttered. The beautiful natural vistas are enhanced by magnificent art and design. Lapland in the north, is a winter sport wonderland, providing activities from reindeer treks to skiing and snow-boarding slopes of every class, and the best of accommodations.

"I am wanting, I am thinking
To arise and go forth singing
Sing my songs and say my sayings,
Hymns of my ancestral harmonizing..."
— from the *Kalevala*

For more information:

For more information about Finnish festivals and organizations, contact the Finnish Tourist Board in New York City. You also can find information about Finnish history and events, both in Europe and North America, on the World Wide Web.

Books by mail:

(Add $4 for shipping and handling. Iowa residents add 5% sales tax. 1998 prices subject to change.)

Suomi Specialties (this book) $12.95
Finnish Proverbs $10.95
FinnFun by Bernhard Hillila $12.95
Fantastically Finnish Recipes and Traditions $9.95
Fine Finnish Recipes $5.95 ($6.95 per copy postpaid)
Words of Wisdom and Magic from the Kalevala $12.95
    (translated by Richard Impola)

Penfield Press, 215 Brown Street, Iowa City, Iowa 52245